Arguments for Socialism

Series editor: John Harrison

Arguments for Socialism is a series of popular and provocative books which deal with the economic and political crisis in Britain today. The series argues the need for a radical rethinking of major political questions and contributes to the debates on strategy for the left.

'One of the main reasons why the Tories swept to power in 1979 was that the Labour movement had over the years almost ceased to argue for socialism. This series, *Arguments for Socialism*, can play a significant part in re-establishing the necessity for a socialism that is democratic, libertarian and humane.' *Tony Benn*

Other **Arguments for Socialism**

Take Over the City: The Case for Public Ownership
of Financial Institutions   Richard Minns

Getting It Together: Women as Trade Unionists
Jenny Beale

More Than We Can Chew: The Crazy World of Food and Farming
Charlie Clutterbuck and Tim Lang

It Makes You Sick: The Politics of the NHS
Colin Thunhurst

The Cuts Machine: The Politics of Public Expenditure
David Hall

Hard Times

The World Economy in Turmoil

Bob Sutcliffe

Pluto Press

First published in 1983 by Pluto Press Limited,
The Works, 105a Torriano Avenue,
London NW5 2RX

British Library Cataloguing in Publication Data
Sutcliffe, Bob   Hard times.—(Arguments for socialism)
1. Depressions—History   2. Economic history   3. Capitalism
I. Title   II. Series
338.5'4   HB3716
ISBN 0-86104-505-X

Cover designed by Clive Challis A Gr R
Cover picture: John Topham Picture Library/John Seymour
Computerset by Promenade Graphics Limited
Block 23a Lansdown Industrial Estate, Cheltenham GL51 8PL
Printed and bound in Great Britain
by Richard Clay (The Chaucer Press) Limited, Bungay, Suffolk

Contents

Acknowledgements / vii

1. Boom and Crisis / 1
The new pessimism / 1
The eclipse of the economics of boom / 3
Crisis and politics / 7

2. Economic Life on the Planet Earth / 9
A wealthy world / 9
Unfair shares / 11

3. The Purple Decades / 16
Capitalism's greatest boom / 16
United States supremacy / 16
Economic internationalism / 18
Capitalist concentration / 21
Jobs, workers and wages / 22
Women's work / 24
The warfare-welfare state / 26
Keynes, Marx and state spending / 27
Unequal development in the third world / 30
The politics of the boom / 32

4. Profile of the Current Crisis / 36
The onset of prolonged crisis / 36
The fall in profits / 38
The impact of the oil crisis / 44
Breakdown of the monetary system / 47

The new protectionism / 49
From growth to stagnation / 50
Profits and unemployment / 51
The new mass unemployment / 53
The unequal burden / 56
The political impact of unemployment / 59
The fiscal crisis of the state / 62
Profits and inflation / 65
Crisis in the third world / 67
Crisis in the 'socialist' states / 70
A world of bad debts / 73
Flashpoints of the crisis / 75

5. The Capitalist Search for a Way Out / 77
The death of consensus / 77
The radical right / 80
Thatcherism / 82
Reaganomics—an inconsistent experiment / 84
The family, the nation and race / 88
Problems of a capitalist solution / 90

6. A Socialist Horizon / 95
Is there another way? / 95
Alternatives in the labour movement / 96
Problems of the new Keynesianism / 98
Problems of nationalisation and planning / 101
Less work, more jobs? / 103
Nationalism and internationalism / 104
Socialism and parliament / 107
Against militarism / 110
An anti-capitalist alliance / 111

A Guide to Reading / 114

Acknowledgements

The following friends and comrades have (knowingly and unknowingly) helped me in various ways to write this book: Merri Ansara, Alice Amsden, Ron Arruda, Paul Auerbach, Sam Bowles, Hugh Brody, Alan Clinton, Bob Cohen, Margery Davies, Jim Devine, Ann Evans, Andrew Glyn, John Harrison, Pierre Imhof, Richard Kuper, Ian McAlman, Arthur MacEwan, Steven Malies, John Miller, Joe Quigley, Dafydd Roberts, Keith Silvester, Anne-Marie Sweeney, Cath Tate, Les Tate, Miranda Tufnell, Nigel Young.

I thank them all.

Parts of this book have appeared before, in article form, in *Socialist Press*, *Socialist Organiser* and *Workers' Socialist Review*.

1.

Boom and Crisis

The new pessimism

A century ago, in 1883, obituaries of capitalism were not uncommon. But despite great depressions and the menace of war, capitalism in those days seems in retrospect to have been still in its prime. It had been responsible for a century of unprecedented economic and technological advance in a few countries; and it seemed to be on the point of remoulding the whole earth in their image.

In that year the body of Karl Marx, the prophet of the doom of capitalism, had scarcely decomposed before that of John Maynard Keynes, who half a century later was to be hailed as the prophet of its salvation, emerged from the womb.

In the century since 1883 wars, revolutions and depressions have periodically threatened to make the obituaries of capitalism come true. Yet, even in the 1930s when the capitalist system seemed terminally afflicted, it hung on to life to flower again after 1945 in the longest and greatest boom in its history. Marx seemed to be superseded and Keynes (by then decomposing in his turn) confirmed.

Yet it is now more than a decade since the world's economy appeared once again to contract a serious ailment which has been increasingly diagnosed as a major crisis of the capitalist system to be compared with the crises of the 1930s or the late nineteenth century.

Many efforts have now been made to prescribe remedies for the mysterious disease but the infection has proved to be very resistant to treatment. As one symptom subsides another seems to get worse. And one underlying symptom has not been significantly relieved anywhere – that is a long-term, and in many countries very severe, decline in the rate of profit on productively invested capital.

This has been so persistent that as time has gone by the older traditional physicians, the economists, have become more and more uncertain and confused and those who dare to propose remedies have had to prescribe increasingly powerful medicines with increasingly terrifying potential side-effects.

Recently a former Chairman of the United States Council of Economic Advisors, Paul W. McCracken warned that 'the free world is at a dangerous juncture where the wrong set of moves could head it towards economic and political disaster'.

Such fearful opinions are now very common among leading figures of the capitalist class and respectable academics. They are a far cry from the general opinions two decades ago when commentaries on the future of capitalism were usually suffused with a bright glow of optimism.

The successors of John Maynard Keynes argued that, given appropriate state intervention in the economy, the problems which had become so severe in the deep slump of the 1930s could be overcome in a capitalist economy of a new more managed kind. The long postwar boom appeared to confirm this perspective.

Though Keynes himself was never so optimistic, his successors said that capitalism had been immunised for ever against major slumps and could therefore expect, given the right government policies, a boundless future free from major economic crises. The most famous economics textbook printed in the postwar period (by the American economist Paul Samuelson) stated: 'Everywhere in the Western world governments and central banks have shown they can win the battle of the slump.' Another prominent economist, Gottfried Harberler, wrote: 'A repetition of the catastrophe of the Great Depression today is practically impossible.'

For a time many people believed that capitalism had, like the adventurers in James Hilton's famous novel *Lost Horizon*, arrived at its Shangri-La, a land of well-being, of growth without ageing, of eternal dynamism. Today, however, the magic of the 1950s and 1960s seems as inaccessible as the valley of Shangri-La.

The eclipse of the economics of boom

Visions of everlasting boom have now given way to a reality of violent economic fluctuations, crises and inexorably mounting unemployment. The old clear cloudless horizon has darkened and closed in. Shangri-La has been lost; and the hard times are back.

So, today the physicians of the Keynesian era no longer extol and prescribe; they question, they bemoan and they spawn pessimistic neologisms. The most common is 'stagflation'; but economists have recently added to crisis vocabulary the 'zero growth economy', the 'zero sum economy' and 'slowth'. Poor Professor Samuelson is reduced to observing sadly that:

> Whatever government does to handle the 'flation' part of our stagflation inevitably worsens in the short term the stagnation part of the problem. That stubborn reality will not go away . . . Likewise whatever government policy does to help the 'stag' part of the stagflation will ineluctably worsen the inflation part of stagflation.

Keynesians predicted a world without inflation and without unemployment. Yet today throughout the capitalist world inflation is rapid and almost out of control and unemployment is heading for the levels of the 1930s. In absolute numbers more people are unemployed today than ever before. It is therefore hardly surprising that Keynesian theory is now deeply discredited.

In the bureaux of London, Washington, Canberra and, until recently, Paris, Keynesians have been given golden handshakes and put out to grass while the born-again traditionalists move in. There has been something of an intellectual counter-revolution and its prophets are Friedrich von Hayek and Milton Friedman. And their respectability is trickling down to economists who twenty years ago would have been dismissed as quacks.

The collapse of the capitalist economy into a prolonged and deep crisis has also contributed to the revival of marxist economics within the capitalist countries (though scarcely yet in the so-called 'socialist' states). Decades after it was buried alive the influence of marxism is beginning to spread once again in the labour movement.

This exhumation of marxist economics is not surprising. Marx's emphasis was not on the equilibrium of the capitalist system but on its inherent contradictions and disequilibrium, on its tendencies not towards stability and continuous expansion but towards crisis and periodic slump. By the early 1970s this seemed to accord much more with reality than either Keynesian or classical bourgeois economics. So did Marx's accent on the role of class struggle rather than the bourgeois vision of a common interest between capital and labour (referred to by many bourgeois economists as the 'social partners'). Even the complaints of the capitalists themselves seemed to bear out Marx's expectations about the falling rate of profit, just as the capitalists' solution – wage cuts and forcing up productivity (output per worker) – seemed to bear out Marx's predictions.

But marxist economics does not exist as a ready-made explanatory or prescriptive formula waiting in the wings to be applied to a new reality. The marxist economics which was written during the boom, as many of its practitioners would today admit, suffered from two apparently different but in fact closely related problems.

The first was a tendency to accept too readily the apparent new stability of the capitalist system and to be blown too far off analytical course by the prevailing Keynesian wind. While, of course, it is easier to make that criticism today with hindsight and a knowledge that the boom was finite, it is nonetheless clear that some of the marxist writings of the boom period failed to see the underlying problems of capitalism behind the boom.

The second problem, or group of problems, also stemmed from the pressure of the boom and the strength which it gave to the new bourgeois ideology of economic optimism. In an attempt to resist this pressure some marxists failed to acknowledge the significance of the boom and the changes in the workings of capitalism which it demonstrated. At the lunatic extreme this involved a few marxists in denying that the boom happened at all or prophesying the end of the boom with the same frequency as religious fanatics prophesy the end of the world. Their error might be described as spitting into the Keynesian wind.

Those two mistakes still infect the search for a satisfactory account of the current crisis of capitalism as a basis for a socialist strategy to combat its pernicious effects. Neither a left sounding description of events nor the restatement of a few theoretical verities from Marx's *Capital* constitute a convincing account of the crisis.

The challenge to socialists today is to bridge the gulf between the concrete events as we experience and perceive them and the theoretical insights into the laws of motion of capitalism which Marx and other socialist theorists discovered. The task is a creative one involving the critical examination of both marxist and bourgeois economic writings, the careful examination and interpretation of concrete facts and the search for the laws behind them, and, based on this analysis, the fight to make the struggle for socialism an effective one.

This book is written from that perspective. But it does not pretend to solve the problems involved in analysing the crisis. Its emphasis is more descriptive than theoretical. And that is partly because I do not believe that the theoretical issues which have been debated among marxist economists in the last decade have yet been resolved to the point where they can simply be applied to illuminate what is happening in the real capitalist world. The light which they cast has often been a rather flickering and dim one.

Too many marxist analyses of the crisis begin with the author's version of Marx's theory of crisis (and the diversity and incompleteness of Marx's work allows for a number of different interpretations) and then go on to give a description of recent capitalist history which is only very tenuously related to the theoretical introduction. Too often theoretical writing has had the same function as wearing a lapel badge saying 'I am orthodox' rather than being a truly creative endeavour.

In this book I have tried to take a different approach. It is structured around a description of what seem to me to be the salient features of postwar capitalism; and it makes periodical brief excursions into the realms of theory in order to help get behind the facts to some of the possible causes.

I have particularly tried to emphasise the qualitative difference between two successive periods of postwar capitalism; the postwar boom of about twenty years during which, with relatively few interruptions, capitalism expanded at a rate without precedent in its whole history; and the subsequent period of prolonged crisis in which growth has been at best erratic and the system has been plagued by chronic problems such as mass unemployment and inflation to which no end is yet in sight.

Some marxists have tended to look at capitalism in this period as if it hung on a weakening thread over a precipice, waiting to collapse imminently into some kind of catastrophe. On the other hand, despite the sometimes very acute problems of the system, no catastrophic collapse has yet occurred. So far at least the events of the crisis have been less apocalyptic than most of us have at times prophesied. We have to try to understand why this is so if we are to be able to devise effective and realistic strategies which will transform this world, in which so many people suffer unnecessary hardship, into a democratic and socialist one in which economic crises need no longer occur.

The account of postwar capitalism in this book does something, though not enough, to try to redress an imbalance of much marxist writing on this subject. This involves a distorted emphasis on events in the advanced capitalist countries. But as a world system capitalism also embraces the underdeveloped countries and their fate is integral to the nature of the crisis.

In addition the interrelations of the capital economies and the economies of the 'socialist' countries of the east has become steadily greater in the postwar period. Now the economic problems of both parts of the world cannot be understood without understanding these interconnections. So I have also tried, albeit very briefly, to integrate this too in the description of the crisis.

My overall hope is that this approach will provide information which will promote further and more informed discussion of the economic crisis among readers, will offer some pointers towards the development of a theoretical understanding of the issues socialists face, and will relate all this to the question of preparing an effective fight for a freer and more just world.

Crisis and politics

But what have economic boom and crisis to do with the possibility of a better world? Some people, such as religious ascetics, have answered: nothing. They say that absolute poverty is the precondition of human fulfilment. At the other extreme much of the propaganda of modern capitalism seems to be based on the idea that human happiness depends on maximising personal consumption.

Probably few of the readers of this book will be tempted by either of these views. But, like its writer, you are likely to be interested in the question of the future of capitalism because of the way it will affect your life and those of others.

For all of us as human individuals, and so for human society as a whole, however it may be socially organised, a satisfactory life requires a certain level of material production in order to provide necessary and useful goods and services – food, wine, houses, medicines, books, radio stations, pianos, electric guitars, and a million other things. And everyone's list would be a bit different.

Because booms and slumps affect the production of all these things then they affect the material preconditions for human survival and fulfilment. But also booms and slumps affect people in a very unequal way. The burden of a slump falls very especially on those who lose their jobs, or have their pay cut, or who are forced to intensify the pace at which they work, or those who are dependent on the goods and services which might be most curtailed, such as health services. Very frequently a slump affects worst those who were relatively disadvan-

taged during better times as well. The already privileged often
suffer the least.

In addition to the changes in the availability of goods and
services between times of boom and slump, human life is
affected also in many more indirect ways. And this is true
especially of a system of production like capitalism in which the
material means of production are not the property of the
members of the society as a whole, but are the sources of
wealth and power of a minority.

In such a society economic booms have often been accompanied by a relaxation of political and social constraints on the
lives of human individuals. Conversely, under capitalism economic crises have usually been associated with the abolition of
some human rights and freedoms. The aftermath of the Great
Depression of the 1930s contained not only mass unemployment and poverty but also in many places the outlawing and
persecution of workers' organisations and that of socialist and
other political groups and parties, the curtailment of rights of
women such as abortion and divorce, the hideous persecution
of Jews, ethnic minorities, homosexuals and many other groups
who could be identified as 'separate', and finally a six-year war
in which tens of millions lost their lives.

Of course it is not easy to establish exactly how these terrible
social and political events were related to the economic ones.
But despite the faults of the view that political events are simply
determined by economic ones few people believe that they
were unconnected in the 1930s and 1940s, or that they are
unconnected today. As a result of the resurgence of major
economic problems in the world, the livelihoods, the freedoms
and even the lives of many of us may be today in grave peril.

2.

Economic Life on the Planet Earth

A wealthy world

It was once possible to study and analyse economic life in one part of the world in isolation from the rest of the planet. Scarcely anywhere is this true today. The economies of the planet earth are more interrelated than ever before. The cause of that more than anything else has been the development of capitalism. One of Marx's insights into the capitalist system was his discovery that, unlike all previous systems of organising production, capitalism has a tendency to expand without limit. That meant that it tended to break down barriers and borders and to create for the first time in history a 'world economy'.

The process has not been even and continuous. Some countries, like the USSR and China, have broken away to some extent from the world capitalist economy; and, especially during crises, capitalist countries have retreated from the rest of the world like snails into their shells in an effort to protect themselves. In such periods world trade and the international division of labour (the extent of specialisation in countries and the exchange of goods between them) has contracted and trade barriers have been erected – a development known as protectionism.

But the long-term trend of capitalism has been towards the increasing international division of labour, towards foreign investment, international markets in commodities, in financial assets, and in some kinds of labour. Those developments have never been faster than in the period of the postwar boom.

A decision to raise the price of oil taken by a feudal monarch in Jeddah might threaten to worsen the balance of payments of the USA which might prompt American central bankers to raise interest rates which might create new problems for a country deep in international debt like Poland which might lead the Polish government to increase meat prices for Polish consumers.

The world economy today is like a complexly patterned fabric composed of long causal threads of which the above is an oversimplified example. At the cost of oversimplifying even more, let us try to look at the world economy as a whole, as if from a great distance.

Imagine viewing the economy of the planet earth from the vantage point of an extra-terrestrial being in an economic observer satellite. How could today's world economy be described?

First of all the value of the total production of goods and services in the world in 1980 – what might be called the 'Gross Planetary Product' – was around $10 trillion (1 trillion = 1,000 billion). Given that the population of the earth is around 4.5 billion that implies that the average value of production per head was $2,222 – that is about two-fifths of the average level for Britain, and about equal to countries such as Argentina, Portugal and Yugoslavia: countries which could be described as the least developed of the developed countries or the most developed of the underdeveloped countries.

Even though there are many reasons why the figure of $2,222 may be inaccurate and misleading, it still possesses great significance. It means, if it is accurate, in even the broadest terms, that the total value of production in the world at the present time – forgetting for a moment what exactly is produced and the way in which it is distributed – is just about enough to sustain a basic standard of life and health for the world's population. If we take into account the fact that many of the world's economic resources are underutilised (both existing means of production and labour) and also that the technical knowledge exists to produce many achievements in the very short run (e.g. the elimination of certain diseases such as malaria) – and if we go beyond that and say that a relatively short-run reallocation of productive resources would make it possible to produce more socially useful products than today – then it is possible to argue an extremely important point: the development of the productive potential of the earth today is sufficient fairly comfortably to meet all the material and many of the cultural needs of its people.

This fact in itself is of no importance at all for capitalists whose only interest is in making profits sufficient to support their existence as an exploiting class, that is a class which materially survives not by producing but by living off the surplus produced by the working class.

For those whom they exploit, however, and for socialists the fact carries immense importance. It shows that the reason why the majority of the population of the world endure poverty, hard labour, cultural deprivation and in hundreds of millions of cases chronic hunger, disease and premature death, is not that the earth is either short of productive resources. Nor is it that the forces of production (the knowledge, skills and material means of production like machines) have not yet been developed enough to meet human needs. Rather, the reason is, quite simply, the exploitative way in which the world's production takes place and the staggeringly unequal manner in which the world's products are distributed.

It is, therefore, no longer impossibly utopian to conceive of a world in which want and deprivation are abolished. So at first glance an extra-terrestrial wellwisher might think that things were not too bad. But, on descending to a lower orbit, she, he or it would begin to experience some nasty surprises.

Unfair shares

The extra-terrestrial observer would first of all be shocked and astonished to see literally billions of people on this rich planet with urgent unfilled needs while millions of people were not working, tens of thousands of factories were closed down and millions of hectares of fertile land left uncultivated.

Our observer would be further perplexed to discover that in

one part of the planet (the so-called third world) 800 million people are suffering from undernourishment (too few calories) and millions of others from malnutrition (deficiencies of essential nutrients). Yet elsewhere the European Economic Community spends $7 billion a year to accumulate unsold stocks of food under its infamous Common Agricultural Policy. And the US government spends billions more to encourage farmers in the USA not to plant food crops.

The E.T. might also be disturbed to notice that spending on the means of destruction (so-called 'defence') in the 18 most developed countries is about $200 billion (and if the Warsaw Pact countries are added that goes up to perhaps $400 billion); at the same time spending on health care in the 36 poorest countries of the world (containing over half its population) was only $5 billion. In fact the poorest countries themselves spend 3½ times as much on the military as they do on health.

It would not take a reasonably bright E.T. observer more than a few orbits to surmise that one of the reasons why the world's productive resources, though quite sufficient to solve the material problems of its people, are not used for that purpose is the way production is organised – that it is by and large motivated for profit or for the power needs of bureaucratic rulers, rather than to fulfil human needs.

This, any sensible E.T. would conclude, is one of the causes of the horrifying unequal way in which consumption is divided between countries and between individuals. A few countries dominate the world economy – broadly speaking those which succeeded in industrialising before the early twentieth century and Japan.

Out of the 'Gross Planetary Product' of $10 trillion no less than 63 per cent is produced in the 18 industrialised capitalist countries, which contain only 16 per cent of the world's population. These are most of the countries of the OECD (Organisation for Economic Cooperation and Development) which will be referred to often in the pages which follow. One country alone, the USA, contains 5 per cent of the world's population but accounts for 25 per cent of planetary production.

By contrast the 36 poorest countries contain 50 per cent of the earth's population and produce only 5 per cent of its product. The 'socialist' economies contain 8 per cent of the world's population and produce 15 per cent of its product. So if we just look at national averages then the national income in the USA per person is over 40 times as high as it is in the 36 poorest countries.

That kind of figure, however, is misleading: it grossly under-estimates the amount of inequality in the world because within the individual countries there are also huge inequalities. In the United States, for example, the wealthiest 10 per cent of the population (over 20 million people) have an average income ten times as high as the poorest 20 per cent of the people. And in Brazil, to give an extreme example, the wealthiest 20 per cent are 67 times better off than the poorest 20 per cent.

So we see here, not for the last time in this book, the deceptive nature of economic averages. The earth's average income of $2,222 per head (in 1980) conceals the fact that the most privileged sections of the people in the advanced capitalist countries are many thousands of times wealthier than the poorest people in the underdeveloped countries. Within nearly all countries these economic differences between individuals are systematically related to the place people occupy in the social hierarchy. In the capitalist west wealth and power are concentrated in the hands of the minority who own and control the means of production and who as a result enjoy many economic privileges. In the 'socialist' east and in many countries in the third world an oversized parasitic bureaucracy often occupies an equivalent privileged position.

Even within the majority who do not own or control the means of production (the working class and middle class) economic, as well as social, discrimination occurs against particular groups. The best jobs available are customarily the preserve of men. Women tend to be forced into inferior jobs, and their level of pay, even in full-time work tends even in advanced capitalist countries to be only between two-thirds and three-quarters of that of men. In white-dominated societies communities of a different colour or of a national minority usually have worse jobs, lower pay, higher unemployment and inferior housing conditions. Open lesbians and gay men find many jobs closed to them due to bigotry. In third world countries differential access to land has a large effect on people's relative economic position – making all the difference between a life of poverty and a death of starvation.

The hierarchy of relative privilege and deprivation in modern economies is immensely complex. Its existence must seem quite unnecessary from the innocent vantage point of the observer satellite from which the earth would appear quite capable of offering a pleasing and generous life to all its inhabitants. In order to understand why, in spite of the potentiality of stable affluence, the economy of earth is characterised by instability and extremes of inequality, an economically curious extraterrestrial would have to descend to the surface of the planet and examine it in more detail.

In fact, our visitor would figuratively have to penetrate beneath the surface of economic life – the productive resources and social needs which are clearly visible – to the motives for production and the obstacles to the rational use of resources to meet the needs which results from these motives. In other words it is necessary to look not just at the economy, but at the *capitalist* economy and the '*socialist*' economy and how they actually function.

Only then can it be discerned that problems of inequality are not purely moral ones which can be redressed by changes of heart; rather the inequalities in distribution and the problems which result from them are part and parcel of the same question as that of how products are produced. It is exploitation in the forms of production which more than anything else results in these inequalities and which means that the world economy reproduces mass starvation, unemployment and chronic disease from day to day and from generation to generation.

It is for this reason, therefore, that socialists have argued that the solution to the economic problem cannot be posed in terms of redistribution alone. The conditions for redistribution can only be created when the nature of production is changed, when exploitative systems are destroyed.

If an international Robin Hood attempted to improve the lot of the poor of the capitalist world by taking from the rich then his endeavour would not last long. For under capitalism greater wealth is the main motive of investment and production. If that motive were made inoperative then much production would cease, unless it could be reorganised under a system with a radically different motive force – one which was not propelled by greed. Under capitalism the value of Robin Hoods is real, but more for the publicity they can give to the problem than for the contribution they are able to make to its solution.

For those who seek a world in which individual human beings can express and develop themselves creatively and be free from want, the purpose of economic and political analysis of today's society is to search for the conditions to end it.

We cannot conduct that search properly by seeing the world statically as a snapshot at one instant. We have to see how it is moving and changing, to see it as a motion picture. Then we can perceive its contradictions and how socialists can help to change it. The next two chapters of the book, therefore, are concerned with the economic history of the last thirty or so years of boom and crisis which have produced the wealth, waste and inequalities which a visiting E.T. would be so amazed to discover.

3.

The Purple Decades

Capitalism's greatest boom

In the postwar world capitalism has developed in astonishingly dramatic and unexpected ways.

In 1945 at the end of the most costly and bloody conflict the world had ever known marxist and bourgeois economists were almost unanimous in predicting that capitalism would re-enter a massive slump equal to or worse than that of the 1930s.

And they were unanimously wrong. By 1950 capitalism had embarked upon a generation of expansion which had never been equalled in its history. The production of goods and services, the productivity of labour, the stock of the means of production, productive technology, the invention of new products, world trade and the international division of labour – all these expanded in the 1950s and 1960s faster, and for a longer sustained period, than ever before in the history of capitalism. The Gross Planetary Product was doubling every 16 years. It is the American writer Tom Wolfe who has named these 'the purple decades', implying a contrast with the grey of the 1930s.

In asserting the significance of this great postwar capitalist expansion we need also to see the changes which were occurring in the structure of capitalism and the problems and contradictions which the expansion produced and this chapter examines some of those.

United States supremacy

In 1945 when the European economies and Japan were still

wracked by the devastation of the war, the physically unscathed United States was the supreme economy of the capitalist world.

United States dominance was shown by the fact that it produced about 70 per cent of the advanced capitalist world's output and accounted for over 25 per cent of its exports of manufactured goods, as well as a high proportion of raw material exports. United States corporations were able to buy up means of production in other countries and US banks loaned money to foreign corporations. The US railroaded through the Bretton Woods conference a new world monetary system which was based on the supremacy of the dollar. The value of the US dollar was fixed in terms of gold (at $35 an ounce) and most other currencies were fixed in relation to the dollar, which also became the currency in which most countries held their reserves. For years afterwards holding dollars was like owning Aladdin's lamp: you could get anything you wanted with them.

The more enlightened sections of the American capitalist class realised very soon after the second world war that such a degree of dominance by the US economy might be self-defeating since in many parts of the world, especially Western Europe, it threatened to force the rest of capitalism into extinction. Within a few years of the end of the war, therefore, they launched an anti-communist political offensive and immediately afterwards began to take measures designed to lead to the capitalist reconstruction of Western Europe and Japan such as Marshall Aid. To maintain capitalism against the threat from the Soviet Union, the US was obliged to sacrifice an element of its dominance and allow Europe and Japan to stand on their own feet.

Since that moment the story has been one of continuous decline in the relative weight of the US in the capitalist system punctuated by movements of crisis in which crucial aspects of its leadership were transformed. The most dramatic of these were the years 1971 to 1974 when the old monetary system based on the almighty dollar was destroyed and the ability of the US to control the rest of the capitalist economy seemed to be severely shaken.

Now the USA produces only 40 per cent of the production of

the advanced capitalist countries in place of 70 per cent in 1945. Its share of world production has gone down from 40 per cent in 1955 to 24 per cent today. And it accounts for only 11 per cent of world exports of manufacturers. Both West Germany and Japan now export more than the USA.

The counterpart of this relative decline of the USA, as well as of Britain, its junior partner, has been the rise in the economic importance of Japan, the Western European countries, especially West Germany, and a few third world countries. In 1950 Japan's GNP per head was only a tenth of that of the USA; today it is about 80 per cent. In the same time West Germany's has gone from a third of the US level to overtake it. Eight Western European countries now have a higher GNP per head than the USA. These developments have meant that the balance of national strength within the imperialist countries has shifted quite considerably since 1950. The shift has been accentuated not only by the economic growth of other imperialist powers relative to the United States, but also by the decline in the overall world power of the USA, as witnessed by defeats in Vietnam, Iran, Africa and so on. This has reduced the weight and credibility of the USA as the overall military and political protector of the whole world capitalist system.

But in spite of this the USA remains the dominant capitalist power. In some ways the figures for the relative size of American production are misleading and underestimate the relative size of US capital since there has been an enormous upsurge of investment by US capitalists in other countries which is part of the vast internationalisation of capital which had occurred. Very recently, this has begun to be counteracted by the start of sizeable Japanese, German and even British investment in the USA. But the generalisation about US dominance still remains true.

Economic internationalisation

The period since the beginning of the great boom has been one of enormous extension of the international interpenetration of capitalist economies. This has taken place in the first instance through the growth of world trade which has been far in excess of the growth of production. World trade grew by 8.6 per cent between 1950 and 1970 while production was growing at 4.9 per cent a year.

Protectionism certainly did not die; but many tariff and other barriers to trade were dismantled, especially between the advanced capitalist countries. This means that there was a great extension of the international division of labour and the capitalist economies became more integrated with each other. Most of this growth was in trade between advanced capitalist countries which now accounts for 54 per cent of all world trade compared with 34 per cent in 1950.

Part of this growing division of labour was not the result of increasing exports by the capitalists of one nation to those of another but was the result of the growth of international investment and the multinational corporation. Much of what appears statistically as trade between two nations actually consists of the movement of semi-finished products, raw materials and so on between different national branches of the same firm. There are various estimates of the extent of this kind of 'transfer trade'. They tend to place it between 25 and 40 per cent of all world trade today.

Twenty-eight per cent of US imports are internal to American multinationals, though most of their production outside the USA is sold within the country where it is produced. It would appear that the search for markets is a much more important motive for American investment abroad than the search for cheap labour.

The internationalisation of capital is also shown by the growth of foreign investment. In 1976 the amount of capital which was owned outside the country in which it operated was estimated by the UN at $287 billion – and of this 94 per cent was owned by the top 11 capitalist countries and 48 per cent by the US alone.

A recent study by the US Department of Commerce estimates that the sales of US multinational corporations alone are $648 billion (nearly 10 per cent of 'Gross Planetary Product') and they employed over seven million people. Production by foreign branches of large multinational corporations ('overseas production') was very high in relation to home production for several major capitalist countries. For six countries (the USA, Britain, Switzerland, Sweden, the Netherlands, and Belgium) the value of such overseas production was more than a fifth as large as their total national income.

The form of the postwar international investment boom has largely been that of investment by capitalists of one advanced country in another and this tendency has been growing. By 1975 three-quarters of the foreign owned capital of the world was in other advanced capitalist countries and only a quarter in the third world. If the oil producing countries and the 'tax haven' countries are excluded then only 17 per cent of all foreign owned capital was in the rest of the third world.

Internationalisation has taken place not only in productive investment but also in the development of banking and financial markets. A vast network of international banks has been established partly to assist the development of capitalist trade and investment throughout the world. This development has literally transformed the shape of the centre of virtually every major city in the world in the postwar period as their characteristic glass towers have competed with each other like the brick towers of medieval Italian nobles. With the growth of these banks has gone the growth of new financial assets and markets. By the second half of the 1970s one-half of the profits of American banks were coming from their foreign operations (compared with less than one-quarter for industrial capitalists).

Most of these new and expanded international banks have been involved in the Euro-dollar market. This is the common, if not completely accurate, name given to the banking system which evolved in the 1960s based on deposits and loans made in US dollars but outside American territory and, therefore, outside American financial control. Since then this market has expanded to include many other major currencies. Deposits in the form of Euro-dollars, virtually out of the control of any state monetary system or central bank now exceed $600 billion, twice the value of all international direct investment.

Some idea of the importance of the international banking

network is given by a recent estimate which put the value of all trading in foreign exchange at $25 trillion a year – 2½ times the total value of world production and 20 times the value of world trade in goods and services.

The internationalisation of capital is related to changes in the form and role of the capitalist state. Along with internationalisation has gone the development and strengthening of what are still rudimentary state institutions at the international level – the GATT (General Agreement on Tariffs and Trade), the IMF (International Monetary Fund), NATO and the EEC. But international capital's needs for the development of internationalised state functions has not been met by these developments; and so institutions and arrangements have been made by the private sector itself. This is part of the function of the Euro-currency market.

Capitalist concentration

In most capitalist countries, mergers and takeovers have led to a very considerable increase in concentration of production in the hands of a few monopolies. And the growth of multinational corporations has meant that this process of concentration has also gone on at a world level. In the USA the biggest 200 manufacturing firms produced 47 per cent of output in 1950 and 60 per cent in 1970. In Britain the top 100 firms produced 22 per cent of output in 1949 and 42 per cent in 1975. In 1977 the top 50 companies owned 33 per cent of all company assets;-the top 250 companies owned almost 60 per cent of assets. In other capitalist countries the figures and trends are similar.

This process of concentration in most countries was a continuous one during the boom. One response to the fall in profitability in the last decade or so has been the acceleration of the trend. In some countries there have been sensational waves of mergers and takeovers.

For instance, in Britain during the 1960s merger boom, firms representing as much as a third of the value of industrial capital were taken over by other firms. The total value of mergers in the United States between 1975 and mid-1981 was $211 billion, around one-twelfth of all American industrial and commercial capital. Within the relatively declining industrial sector recent bankruptcies and financial crises are probably leading to faster concentration than ever.

Jobs, workers and wages

The postwar boom led to an immense expansion of the size of the working class. In Western Europe and Japan the remnants of pre-capitalist systems in agriculture were broken down. Agriculture was brought increasingly under capitalist production relations; many workers were driven off the land in this process and drawn into wage employment in the cities. In the 25 years starting in 1950 the proportion of workers in agriculture in the advanced capitalist countries fell from 22 per cent to less than 8 per cent. Correspondingly the proportion in industry expanded (except in the USA and Britain); and the proportion in the services sector expanded everywhere without exception.

In the less developed parts of the capitalist system the pace of industrialisation was not enough to provide jobs for all but was enough to bring millions of workers into wage employment. Millions of them also migrated to the imperialist countries to become the most underprivileged section of the workforce there. And millions of women were brought into wage employment while in previous generations they had been occupied entirely in work in the home (see below).

The expansions of wage employment, however, had contradictory aspects. A great deal of it was not employment under strict capitalist relations but rather employment in the rapidly expanding state sector of the advanced capitalist economies. This fact is linked with the type of jobs which expanded most in the boom – service sector jobs in both the public and private sectors.

In many countries this meant especially the growth of local authority jobs. In Britain, for instance, between 1959 and 1974 total employment rose by 6 per cent. Private sector employment rose by only 3 per cent in this period, while local authority jobs expanded by 60 per cent, bringing public employment up to nearly one-third of the total. The boom also saw a striking increase in the organisation of the working class into trade unions. In Britain, for instance, the membership of the TUC affiliated unions went up from 7.9 million in 1945 to 12.4 million 30 years later (a rise from 39 per cent to 52 per cent of the labour force). In Belgium, the Netherlands and Scandinavia a similar rise took place. In France and Italy, however, union membership dropped very sharply from their peak immediately after the 1945 liberation; the numbers in unions only started to rise again in the late 1950s.

In the USA unionisation rose, at its peak in the early 1950s, to only 26 per cent of the workforce and has since then fallen to around 20 per cent. Organised labour in the USA was unable to break the vicious anti-union policies of many of the most rapidly growing US monopolies. The ubiquitous IBM, for instance, is a non-union company; so are Polaroid, Hewlett-Packard, Grumman, Eastman-Kodak, Gillette and Texas Instruments.

In nearly all countries, the combination of relatively full employment, fast economic growth and increased union organisation produced steady rises in wages in money terms and for the most part in real terms too in the two decades after 1950. Again, the USA is a partial exception: there, real wages reached their peak in 1967 and since then have been falling. (The real wage is a measure of how much a worker can buy with her or his wage. If there is inflation real wages rise slower than money wages.)

During the 1950s the regular wage contract (usually annual or every two or three years) became a regular feature for most workers in the imperialist countries whereas in most countries between the wars wage demands, let alone increases, had been a rare occurrence.

This tendency towards greater and greater consciousness of the real wage and a more and more militant attitude towards defending it was heightened by the continuous though still slow inflation during the postwar period. In three countries, France, Belgium and Italy, workers' struggles succeeded in winning a considerable degree of protection of wages against inflation – a limited sliding scale in which wages were automatically raised when prices increased.

But in all these countries such developments have made wage conflicts between the working class and employers or the state more and more frequent, and national conflicts and strikes a commonplace happening.

Women's work

Changes in the position of women have been among the most striking during the course of the boom. First of all women have been drawn into the commercial labour force on a larger scale than ever before.

In the main capitalist countries (i.e. the OECD members) the proportion of the male population aged 15–64 which was in the labour force fell from 95 to 86 per cent in the two decades after 1960. But the proportion of women who were in the labour force rose from 46 to 53 per cent. In the USA 6 out of 10 women are in the labour force and in Scandinavia more than 7 out of 10. Most of this growth in what is known as the labour force 'participation rate' was the result of the number of married women with paid jobs. For instance, in 1950 only one out of five married American women had a paid job; in 1980 the proportion was more than one in two.

This entry to the labour force has been tied up with many of the new forms of white collar employment which have burgeoned along with the growing economic role of the state. So the incorporation of women into the labour force has gone along with the creation of new areas which are in practice considered to be 'women's work', rather than with greater equality of access to men's jobs.

This means that despite equal pay legislation in a number of countries including Britain, women's pay continues to be lower than men's by a substantial margin, even in full-time employment. This is because even the new generation of 'women's jobs' are less well paid and very often entail worse conditions of service than men's employment. In the USA women comprise over 90 per cent of secretaries, cleaners, servants, nurses, key punch operators, sewers and stitchers, bank tellers and telephone operators. In Europe the situation is similar.

These changes have been accompanied by a relative decline of the extended family and the further rise of the nuclear family as the standard living unit, a development which has made substantial changes to the way individuals and families fit into the capitalist economic structure. More and more families have depended on receiving two regular wage incomes.

Public and private housing developments have helped to enforce the nuclear family through the regulations imposed by public housing authorities and mortgage companies for eligibility for homes and loans. Sometimes services previously provided within the home have been socialised. And very often it has been women workers who have been paid to provide the services.

The mechanisation of housework in advanced countries has meant that very large areas of capitalist production have been directed towards supplying (and creating) the needs of households – refrigerators, washing machines, heating systems and countless gadgets; and the detergents and convenience foods to go with them. Through the ubiquitous TV set 'the housewife' has become the number one victim of capitalist advertising and the number one subject of male politicians' platitudes.

Writers from the women's movement have emphasised how the changing role of women (especially working-class women) in the postwar advanced economies has not by and large resulted in greater independence. Women's unchanged role in the home as the 'slave of slaves' has been combined with expanding opportunities for wage employment often in the lowest paid areas of service work. In the USA a survey has shown that women with paid jobs still do 25 hours of housework a week on average.

It is not surprising, therefore, that the boom had the particular effect of heightening awareness of the oppression of women and resulted in the development of the largest political movement of women in history. This movement was not confined to the advanced countries. But in the third world neither the workers' nor the women's movement has been strong enough to prevent the growth of a new super-exploited female work-force in the fast growing Newly Industrialising Nations of South-east Asia, in industries like micro-electronics.

The warfare-welfare state

Probably the key difference between capitalism in the post-war boom and all previous epochs of capitalism has been the growth and change in the economic role of the state. The American writer James O'Connor has appropriately called it the 'warfare-welfare state'.

State production has expanded enormously, especially in Europe, as a result of the wave of nationalisations which took place in the aftermath of the war and less frequently since then. Nationalised industries have been used by the state both in policies to manage the level of demand and wages in the economy and indirectly to influence the position of capitalist industry via nationalised industry pricing policy, purchasing policy and so on. State procurement by nationalised industries, as well as in other areas of state expenditure, has also become one of the major new forms of protectionism.

There has also been an expansion of the traditional forms of expenditure of the state on the armed forces, weapons and the rest of the repressive apparatus concerned with law enforcement.

Military expenditure by the capitalist countries in general, though proportionately lower than in wartime, has in the whole of the postwar period been higher than ever before in peacetime – higher in relative terms as a proportion of total national income, and so immensely higher in real terms. Military spending by NATO and the Warsaw Pact in 1980 was about equal in value to the whole national income of the world's poorest 36 countries, containing half the world's population. In other words the diversion of military spending to useful purposes could in principle double the income of half the people of earth.

Despite the grotesque size of arms and military spending, the major growing areas of state spending have been such publicly provided services as health, education and social welfare –

including grants like unemployment and social security benefit. The total of government spending on goods and services and these so-called 'transfers' has risen in Japan and the USA to over 30 per cent of the value of national income; in Western European countries typically to around 45 per cent; and exceptionally in Holland and Sweden to over 60 per cent.

In Britain welfare spending rose from 16 per cent of the national income in 1951 to 29 per cent in 1975 and this is quite typical of the rest of the advanced capitalist world. In the rest of Western Europe welfare spending was somewhat higher than in Britain; in the USA slightly lower. Only in Japan among the advanced countries was it considerably less.

Keynes, Marx and state spending

It is impossible to understand the working of postwar capitalism without appreciating the role of this vastly expanded state spending. That is not so easy since there is a good deal of conflict among 'experts' about whether such high levels of state spending help or harm the capitalist economy. The battles rage among both supporters and opponents of capitalism.

In the Keynesian era state expenditure and 'demand management' became widely regarded as an elixir of youth for capitalism – a kind of monkey gland treatment which would keep the limbs supple and the skin soft. The problem was that it didn't do much for the heart of the system – profitability which, as we shall see in detail in the next chapter, declined as the boom wore on.

Even the most hardcore Keynesians have now become perplexed by the strange combination in the 1970s of rising relative and absolute state expenditures, rising unemployment and high inflation. Keynesian expectations were always that the capitalist economy offered a trade-off between inflation and unemployment (that is, the more you had of one the less you were supposed to get of the other).

The failure of Keynesians to solve this economic Rubik's cube and produce an explanation of simultaneous inflation and unemployment has help to open up space for the new economic

right. Many pro-capitalist economists today reject Keynesianism and argue that state spending, beyond what is absolutely
necessary for law enforcement and so on, is unambiguously
damaging to the capitalist economy. Many different arguments
are used, in various permutations, to back up this view; that
high state spending fuels inflation, holds up interest rates, and
so cuts back productive investment, 'crowds out' private spending in other ways, or reduces 'enterprise' and other alleged
capitalist virtues; or that taxes to finance high government
spending are a drain on private profits. From those elements
could be put together an identikit picture of the views of almost
any modern right-wing economist.

These disputes about how to analyse the role of state spending are the background to the sharp conflicts now going on
within the main political forces of the leading capitalist countries about economic policy. They are dealt with in Chapter 5
below.

The analytical disputes, however, are not restricted to the
corridors of power or the salons of the ruling class. They rage
also among socialists, though the terms of the debate may be
rather different.

Marx analysed capitalism before state spending was very
important; but his basic approach to all economic questions,
which has been followed by later marxists, was to examine the
effects of economic phenomena on the ability of capitalism to
reproduce itself through the making of profit and the continuous accumulation of capital. Capitalism can survive only by
accumulating (or re-investing) profits. And these profits arise
only if two conditions are simultaneously met: first, in the
course of capitalist production workers must create goods and
services which contain more value (or more human labour
time) than the value of the machines, materials and labour used
up in production; second, the goods and services which are
produced must be sold on the market for a price which is
equivalent to their value. Marx gave these two necessary parts
of profit-making the technical names of the production and
realisation of surplus value. Since the resulting surplus goes not
to the workers who produce it by their labour but to the

capitalists who appropriate it due to their property then the whole system of profit-making is one of exploitation.

The question for marxists is: how does state spending relate to this process of capitalist exploitation and accumulation? And marxists have given very varying answers to that question. Some argue that state expenditure does not help to produce surplus value but is on the contrary a drain on it and is therefore detrimental to the interests of capital. The problem with that point of view is that it fails to account for why the increase in spending has taken place and can ascribe it to little other than capitalist irrationality. It is more accurate to say that some state spending enters directly into the reproduction of capital by providing necessary services, especially to the production of labour power. This part of state spending, including some education and health services, has often been called the 'social wage'. In addition other portions of state spending contribute indirectly to the reproduction of capital, such as research and development expenditure, road building and maintenance, the construction of power stations, and so on. Further parts of state spending represent the growing costs of reproducing capitalist social relations – of making exploitation 'acceptable', either through propaganda and welfare schemes or through law enforcement and repression.

But it would be wrong to see state spending as entirely serving some function in relation to the needs of capitalism. A certain amount of it has been wrested from capitalist governments by mass pressure of the working class and has clearly represented concessions which the capitalist class has been obliged to pay for the political survival or stability of the system. The contradictions produced by these concessions have become plain only with the onset of the crisis and are discussed in Chapter 4 below.

At one stage capitalist governments connived in the expansion of state spending whereas now almost everywhere they attempt to reduce it; even so, there remain some sections of the capitalist class which do not oppose it because they live on it (for example the builders of hospitals and publishers of school textbooks). This fact suggests a dual and contradictory function which state expenditure performs for capitalism. And that can be very well explained in relation to something else which Marx stressed strongly in this theoretical writings on capitalist crisis – that there is a contradiction between the *production* of surplus value and its *realisation*.

Different forms of state spending contribute both to the production and realisation of surplus value. But much of state spending has a more contradictionary role: it assists the realisation of surplus value by maintaining high demand for goods and services (and it is this aspect which was stressed by Keynesians); yet at the same time its financing demands one way or another a subtraction from surplus value produced (which is the aspect stressed by the anti-Keynesians).

If we accept the combined and contradictory role of state spending then it would appear that the Keynesians and anti-Keynesians, along with those marxists who take one-sided views of the question, have all arrived only at half-truths. They stress different, individually correct but insufficient aspects of the whole truth. Unfortunately two half-truths tend not to add up to one whole truth. And when it comes to a guide for action half a truth may not be any better than no truth at all.

But even to realise that state spending both benefits the process of capital accumulation and hinders it at the same time does not, at such a level of generality, answer the specific problems that are posed. In particular it does not explain why rising state expenditure during the boom seemed generally acceptable to capitalism while in the 1970s high state spending emerged suddenly and almost universally as a major problem. This particular puzzle will be partly unravelled in the section on the fiscal crisis of the state in Chapter 4 and will also be dealt with in the final chapter in the discussion about the struggle over economic policies within and between capitalist governments.

Unequal development in the third world

The capitalist boom had profound effects on the underdeveloped countries of the third world. Both a lack of accurate statistics and the variety of their experience makes it impossible to generalise too much. Yet it is probably true to say that the economic gulf between the rich and poor capitalist countries grew greater during the boom. That is not to say that the boom did not extend to the underdeveloped countries. In fact on average they experienced a faster rate of growth of production than the advanced capitalist countries. It was not fast enough, however, to redress the imbalance caused by differential rates of population growth. So the average income per head in the poorer countries, while it grew, fell further back in relation to the developed ones.

But an average as we have seen can be very misleading. In fact in the third world there have been boom countries, even if sometimes the booms have been concentrated in one city, and others which have experienced absolute economic decline.

Statistically the most successful countries have been the half dozen oil producers, which are in a class by themselves, and another half dozen countries which in the 1960s began to export manufactured goods on a large scale (for example, Taiwan, Singapore, South Korea, Hong Kong, Brazil).

Success was usually based on the tightest possible repression of the growing industrial working class (especially of women workers) and often represents not the independent capitalist development of the countries concerned but rather the geographical expansion of capital from the more advanced countries. Nonetheless a number of Asian and Latin American countries now have quite large local industrial sectors and large domestic markets for manufactured goods. Foreign investment has recently gone to such countries (for example Mexico, Brazil, Korea and Taiwan) not so much in search of cheap labour as of rich markets. The boom brought a few such countries close to the status of developed industrialised countries.

The spread of political independence of the colonies after the end of the war led in most third world countries to a huge expansion of the state military and bureaucratic apparatus, which has been responsible for draining a vast surplus from the people in support of material privileges and which, being parasitic on the people, has developed in collaboration with economic aid – both from capitalist and 'socialist' countries.

It is this bureaucracy which has been the stumbling block of many an economic plan which could have spread the benefits of better technology to the poor especially in the countryside. Even when important technological developments have taken place – such as the much heralded 'green revolution' produced by the development of new high-yielding varieties of rice and wheat – the benefits have been aborted, the mass of peasants losing out.

Many recent studies have agreed that the development of the third world has involved the further impoverishment of literally hundreds of millions of people. The growth of relatively automatic state benefits to cover unemployment and destitution has been restricted to a few advanced countries. Socialist writers like Andre Gunder Frank have clarified how today's underdevelopment is not just an aboriginal state akin to that of the developed countries a century or more ago. It is not a state from which the underdeveloped countries can now develop in their turn with all the benefits of being latecomers. It is more that the features of modern underdevelopment have been *created* in the course of the unequal development of world capitalism. And they constitute a serious obstacle to the development of poor countries. Underdevelopment for the majority is in many ways a necessary counterpart to development for the minority.

While absolute poverty and deprivation have grown in virtually every third world country, a few have experienced a terrifying process of economic decline, especially when afflicted with wars and 'natural' disasters. This is the case for example in West Africa where a prolonged drought has led in a few countries to years of growing economic catastrophe and starvation on a mass scale.

The politics of the boom

In the advanced capitalist countries of North America, Western Europe and Japan the typical political regimes of the great postwar boom have been forms of parliamentary democracy.

The history of the period is not short of major attacks on

democratic rights such as the McCarthyite anti-communist witch-hunts in the United States in the early 1950s, the *Berufsverbot* (the law which prohibits suspected communists from holding jobs in the public service) in West Germany, the coming to power of de Gaulle and his imposition of a much less democratic constitution in France in 1958, and the introduction of racist anti-immigration controls in Britain. And even by the end of the boom many elementary freedoms were still withheld in many countries. Laws and customs existed which supported discrimination against people not of the dominant race or colour of the country in question, against women (especially in the areas of abortion and contraception), against lesbians and gay men and against young people.

But even though a catalogue of limitations to or attacks on democratic freedoms might be endless, the essence of the politics of the period consisted in the maintenance and extension of a form of bourgeois democracy. The preservation of universal suffrage and parliamentary democracy in all the major capitalist countries for more than a generation is a fact without historic precedent. Despite numerous obstacles placed in its way, political and industrial organisation in most advanced capitalist countries flourished. In most countries the trade unions grew in membership and activities. Political parties also flourished. The major electoral parties – those of the bourgeoisie as well as the various socialist, labour and communist parties – grew into mass organisations with greater participation in aggregate than ever before.

For much of the period of the boom the parties of the bourgeoisie managed to rule 'by consent', that is through regular constitutional elections. In Europe, however, they only managed to gain electoral majorities by accepting some of the liberal reforms which their more progressive opponents had advocated. But also for appreciable periods of the boom professedly socialist parties governed major capitalist countries in Europe. Regardless of any radical sounding elements of their programmes they confined themselves to managing, with a few reforms and adjustments, the capitalist system which they found themselves in charge of.

The conditions of the boom therefore produced something of a coagulation of policies and principles between the big electoral parties nominally of right and left. It was a common and only half humorous claim that it was impossible to tell them apart. In Britain a political commentator coined the term 'Butskellism' (combining the name of the Conservative Chancellor of the Exchequer R. A. Butler, with that of Labour Chancellor Hugh Gaitskell) and it immediately became widely used as an accurate description of this new political consensus.

Mass electoral politics, therefore, tended to produce disillusion and cynicism. Seldom had people been asked to vote so often and seldom had it seemed to make less difference. The results of elections were analysed by 'experts' less in terms of policies than in terms of the rival merits of public relations consultants and the television make-up of the leading candidates. So in the new golden age of parliamentary democracy the most powerful and significant mass political movements were for the most part extra-parliamentary ones – the black and anti-Vietnam war movements in the USA, the occasional great strike waves such as in France in 1968 and in Italy in the hot autumn of 1969, the women's and gay liberation movements. Those with particular interests to pursue mobilised for them independently of the parliamentary parties.

The governments of the parliamentary parties of both left and right responded to, or tried to stave off, the growth of autonomous movements by introducing the set of reforms which have come to be known as the welfare state. They consisted of the various combinations of state-provided health-care facilities, schools and colleges, many kinds of social welfare services, public housing, the right to old age pensions, unemployment pay and various state grants to supplement low incomes, already described.

Many of these reforms had never existed before in the history of capitalism. They have played a major role in the consensus politics of the boom and in the ideological defence of the modern capitalist system. In most countries they have been enshrined in legislation which is hard to change. In the United States they are known by the useful name of 'entitlement programmes'. Their existence, the legacy of the boom, radically changes the way in which the present crisis has developed – as will be explained in the following chapter – and radically constrains capitalist governments in their attempts to reverse it.

4.

Profile of the Current Crisis

The onset of prolonged crisis

The boom was not converted into crisis on one day or by a single event like the shattering Wall Street crash of October 1929. Over a period of years the generation of relatively successful capital accumulation, expansion of production and relatively full employment gave way to a distinct new capitalist epoch first of falling profits, contracting capital accumulation, monetary and fiscal crisis, and then increasingly of rising mass unemployment and soaring debt.

It is important to realise that this is not the crisis of one nation or even the capitalist class of one nation. Its symptoms are observable in virtually every individual capitalist country. Other manifestations are international by their very nature, such as the stagnation of world trade. There is, therefore, no possibility that it can be solved at the level of one nation, or that one country can insulate itself from it.

It is also important to recognise that the crisis has not been caused by the erroneous policies of capitalist governments. It is true that the policies of governments sometimes exacerbate some of the consequences of the economic crisis such as inflation and unemployment. But it is the existence of a crisis for which there is no simple solution which provokes governments to follow the policies they do.

Certainly one of the reasons for the drawn-out nature of the present crisis is the nature of the intervention of the state. The state has taken numerous actions to 'alleviate' effects of the crisis which in a previous epoch of capitalism would have occurred naturally. It has, for example, propped up industries which would ōtherwise have gone bankrupt. In spite of the rapid spread of mass unemployment today, state intervention of this kind and others has had the effect, especially during the early stages of the evolution of the crisis, of maintaining employment *above* the level which would have been dictated by the free market.

The other related influences on prolonging the crisis have been the historically unprecedented gains won by the working class during the boom. Such things as the right to unemployment benefit and social security, the partial protection of such benefits against inflation and so on – the entitlement programmes – have been defended by the working class, and capitalist governments have been unable fully to remove them. This means that governments have been unable to impose the degree of cost on the working class necessary to resolve quickly the capitalists' crisis of profitability and accumulation.

This is not to say costs have not been imposed on the working class. The growth of mass unemployment, especially in the last three years, the attack on real wages, and the erosion of social services have all been considerable. They have not yet, however, been sufficient to make any major impact on the problem of profitability which, in spite of a number of short term fluctuations, has nowhere begun to show any sustained tendency to rise again.

These points imply a certain view of the economic crisis:

First, that it is basically a crisis of profitability of capitalism and that its other aspects – the fiscal problems of the state, the energy crisis, the international monetary problems and so on – follow from that fact and are not primary.

Second, that in principle the crisis can be resolved, in the sense that the conditions for profitable accumulation of capital can be restored.

Third, that the process of restoring these conditions is a very painful one which must involve the rationalisation of the structure of capital and the devaluation or destruction of some capital currently participating in the search for a limited quantity of surplus value (profit). And at the same time, it must involve a major worsening in the living standards, conditions and rights of the working class.

Fourth, that this capitalist solution will produce a tendency towards a confrontation of the classes as capitalists attempt to wrest back concessions which have been made. This does not necessarily mean a single decisive class battle, such as a 1926 General Strike or a 1933 Nazi seizure of power. If the attack on the working class is to succeed through attrition, however, then this is bound to be a long drawn out and tortuous process.

Fifth, historical parallels suggest that an outcome which is favourable to capital may both entail the strengthening of political reaction of all kinds – nationalism, racism and sexism – and also heighten the danger of war.

These are the general contours of the crisis in the abstract. To understand it more fully and to link that understanding with the fight for a socialist outcome, it is necessary to look at its more concrete details – to see the way it affects the material conditions, interests and consciousness of those who are destined to act it out.

The fall in profits

When some economists began to assert more than ten years ago that a long-term decline of profitability was taking place this fact was very hotly contested.

In the first place it was contested by pro-capitalist economists who wished to deny that any serious defect was showing up in the system they supported. But secondly, it was also disputed by many socialists. The opposition to the idea came on the one hand from marxists who had under the impact of the boom developed a semi-Keynesian view of the capitalist economy which led them to believe that it could no longer descend into the deep crises characteristic of the pre-Keynesian era. Also opposition came from those whose view of socialism, revolutionary as it sometimes sounded, conceived of the anti-capitalist struggle as basically a moralistic one concerned above all with redistribution from the rich capitalists to the poor workers.

The idea that the whole basis of capitalism, the pursuit of profit, could be upset was unpalatable to those holding both these views. It was also unpalatable to the traditional reformist working-class leaders whose whole political life depends on the ability to hold out the prospects of things getting better under the pressure of reforming 'socialist' governments. The idea that there had been a severe and hard-to-reverse decline in profitability was indigestible because it held out only the possibility that the capitalists would be obliged to make things a whole lot worse.

As the weight of evidence for the fall in profitability mounted, however, the fact came to be more widely accepted, apart from the few who preferred the interpretation that it was a capitalist deception to justify economic austerity to workers. Discussion then was less over *whether* the fall had occurred but *why* and the closely linked question, what could be done about it.

One of the most common approaches towards explaining the fall in profitability is to stress the role of intensifying international competition and the uncompetitiveness of industry in the worst-hit nations like Britain and Italy in relation to other capitalist rivals. In recent years this approach has often gone along with emphasis on the problem of de-industrialisation, the erosion of Britain's or America's industrial base and so on.

The main problem with this approach is that it is at most capable of explaining only a portion of the truth. There is now overwhelming evidence to show that the decline in profitability, though uneven between capitalist nations, is a worldwide phenomenon. There is, of course, a connection between international competitiveness and relative rates of profit in different countries. But this approach is not so good at explaining falls in the rate of profit both in those countries whose industry is becoming less competitive *and* in those whose industry is becoming more competitive. The approach is one which not surprisingly leads to very nationalistic kinds of solution and often conceives of the possibility that British or Italian capitalism are capable, with the right degree of state assistance, of performing as well as German or even Japanese capitalism.

The conditions of international competition, therefore, can explain a lot and need to be studied in order to understand the crisis but they cannot fully explain the decline in the rate of profit, though, if there has been a significant increase in the intensity of competition in the capitalist world as a whole (and this is almost impossible to measure), then this could have played some part in the international fall in profitability.

Another controversial area in explaining the causation of the decline in the rate of profit is the role of the working class. Some socialists tend to argue defensively that the level of wages and the action of the working class in the events which led up to the crisis have played no role in the causative process. This is in part a reaction to various ideological assaults which seek to blame the very existence of the crisis on the excessive greed of the working class.

Although this ideology needs to be combated, the position which says that the level of wages is a purely passive variable in the economic system, which can be omitted from the causal chain, is in fact another version of an argument put forward by some right-wing economists such as Milton Friedman, which says that wages are simply a price, responsive to forces of supply and demand in the market.

Another version of the defensive argument says that the role of trade unions and class struggle over wages had been no more than to ensure that money wages keep up with inflation and thus cannot be seen as an independent causative factor. But in fact it is of crucial importance for the economic situation of capitalism whether or not workers are able through their struggle to prevent the erosion of the real wage through inflation.

It is of course true that class struggle over wages and all other questions such as work conditions plays a crucial role in the position of individual capitalists and of the capitalist economy as a whole. To explain the role of class struggle a brief theoretical digression is needed.

The rate of profit (how much profit capitalists make as a proportion of the value of the capital they have invested) can be seen as the outcome of the interplay between two ratios. The first is the ratio between the two component parts of the value of a product – the old value (or dead labour as it is sometimes called) already embodied in machines and raw materials; and the new value (or living labour) which is added to the old in each production process. That ratio of old to new value (sometimes called the organic composition of capital) is relevant to determining the rate of profit because profits arise only from living labour, and yet some capital has to be invested in old value in order to produce them.

Not all of the value created by living labour is profit. Some of it has to pay the living labourers – that is, the wages of the workers who produce it. So the second important ratio is the division of this new value between capitalists and workers. This is what Marx called the rate of exploitation or rate of surplus value.

Since the rate of profit is determined both by the organic composition of capital and by the rate of exploitation (or surplus value), workers' struggles (which affect the rate of surplus value) must play a significant role in the determination of the rate of profit. But the role and the direction of causation is certainly not a simple one, partly because the effect of wages on profits is a contradictory one rather like state expenditure. (See Chapter 3 above.)

This contradiction can again be best understood by seeing the need for capitalists simultaneously to produce and realise surplus value. A rise in the level of wages makes the production of surplus value more difficult because it raises costs of production; but it makes the realisation of surplus value easier because it raises demand. This contradiction faces capital as a whole, though in some cases it may show up most in the form of division between sections of capitalists. Marx referred to it by pointing out how all capitalists want the wages of their own workers to be low and those of all other capitalists to be high.

So the defensiveness of many socialists on this question of the role of the working class is misplaced. To accept that wages play a major role in the causative chain that results in economic crisis is not to accept that in any sense wage rises are 'to blame' for the crisis.

The effect of wages is complex and contradictory. And their

movement is not a purely independent phenomenon: it is affected by the movement of the capitalist economy itself. There is very powerful evidence to support the idea that once the vast pool of unemployed and underemployed labour after the war was used up by the major capitalist economies, the low level of the reserve army of labour strengthened the bargaining position of trade unions on wages and other questions to a degree which was unacceptable to the capitalist class and which threatened further profitable accumulation.

Capitalists moved onto the offensive in order to increase the rate of surplus value (through a variety of means including inflation and the more conscious one of wage control); the organisational strength of the trade unions then has been decisive in making this solution more difficult for the capitalist class.

It does not follow from this that if the working class had agreed to the level of wage increases demanded by the capitalists then the crisis would not have occurred and the long boom could have continued forever to the mutual benefit of all classes. It would have meant rather that the manifestations of the crisis would have been different. They might have taken the form of a lack of sufficient consumer demand which appears to have been a major problem in the later 1920s.

A further problematic factor in explaining the rate of profit is the role of the organic composition of capital. This has been the centrepiece of much debate among marxist economists in the last decade, the outcome of which has been disappointingly arid, especially in terms of consequences for political strategy. It has been common to present a crude argument which is the counterpart of the defensive argument over wages. This is that the decline of the rate of profit is entirely the result of an increase in the organic composition of capital – and so if it is anybody's responsibility, it is that of the capitalists themselves. This is often combined with an implicit suggestion that marxist theory of economic crisis is basically an extension of what Marx called the law of the tendency of the rate of profit to fall. This is the opposite way round from what Marx himself intended. In his sketches for what would presumably have become a whole volume of *Capital* on crisis it is clear that he considered the fundamental theoretical question in crisis theory to be the contradiction between the production and realisation of surplus value, and that the tendency of the rate of profit to fall was but one of the laws of motion governing the rate of profit.

It must be admitted from a marxist point of view a gap exists which needs to be filled between explanations of crises at the most abstract level – that they manifest the basic anarchy of capitalist production and the contradiction between social production and private appropriation – and the many detailed empirical studies of the crisis and its manifestations. The bridging of that gap is a creative challenge to socialists.

It has now been established to the satisfaction of virtually everyone (except those who disbelieve all statistics published by capitalist governments), that a massive decline in the rate of profit has occurred – and in virtually every major capitalist country. This question has now been so widely studied – a bibliography on it would run to hundreds of pages – that it is only necessary here to give the briefest summary of what has occurred.

In every major capitalist country there has been a pronounced decline in profitability since 1960, in many cases accelerating over the last decade. Some studies suggest that the USA has been an exception, though the most recent ones show it following the international trend. The cut in the rate of profit has been particularly pronounced in Britain, Italy and West Germany. In the advanced capitalist countries as a whole the profit rate in commerce and industry halved in the fifteen years after 1960.

The most recently published international comparison of profit rates suggest that there has been no significant improvement of profitability anywhere in the 1970s. The study shows that between the first and second half of the 1970s there was a further pronounced fall in profitability in Britain and France, a small fall in Japan and West Germany and very little change in the USA.

The available statistics suggest that in most countries the fall in the rate of profit has resulted from two adverse trends: the value of capital invested for each unit of output has risen; and the share of profits relative to wages in the net value of production has fallen. But the second tendency has been much more marked. To revert to the terminology of Marx, it would seem that the rate of exploitation has been falling; and that the organic composition of capital has risen but not so strikingly.

That particular conclusion would not be agreed with by all marxist economists. But most economists of all persuasions would now agree that the very significant fall in the rate of profit which has occurred now constitutes a fundamental problem for the whole capitalist system. Profit is the life-support system of capitalism; and if it is cut off death will be quick but painful. Capitalism is therefore struggling for its life as it always does in a major economic crisis. This does not imply that it is fragile and infirm and can be easily toppled. But it does imply that its continued existence – and even more its health – depends on reversing the adverse trends which developed during the long boom. Most of the dramatic economic events of the last decade or so can be understood best if we see them, partly at least, as either the outcome of the fall in the rate of profit, or as results of efforts made to reverse that fall.

The fall in profitability cannot mechanically explain everything. But if socialists do not see its underlying importance they will be very stunted in their ability to interpret what has happened and to see what might come next. They will therefore be politically weakened.

The impact of the oil crisis

The four-fold oil price increase of 1973–74 was not the basic cause of the capitalist crisis which began long before that. It is intermittently convenient for some capitalists and the more nationalistic labour and trade union leaders to claim that it was the cause since then the 'blame' can be laid at the feet of foreigners. In fact the ability of the OPEC countries to raise the oil price four-fold at a stroke depended on the economic situation in the main capitalist countries. In particular the excess demand in the world oil market resulted from the conversion of the USA in a few years from being self-sufficient in oil to being a large-scale oil importer.

The huge increase in oil prices in 1973–74 had an immediate and very great impact; first, on the international distribution of surplus value appropriated by states, vastly increasing the income of the OPEC nations; second, on the relative strength of capitalist firms, greatly strengthening the already gigantic oil companies; third, on the overall level of world capitalist demand, reducing it because of the hoarding of OPEC balances which were not all recycled (that is, lent back to the consuming countries rather than hoarded); and fourth, on the balance of payments of various parts of the world leading to huge deficits for several years in advanced capitalist countries and persistently in underdeveloped countries, thereby strengthening an extra protectionist and deflationary bias in economic policy. These effects have continued since then even though the oil price in real terms was eroded over the period from 1974–80. Then again in 1980–81, the oil price more than doubled, reinforcing the problem, though under the impact of prolonged slump conditions the price had begun to collapse again by the spring of 1981 with as yet unforeseeable effects.

OPEC today no longer wields the power which it had in 1973. Then it controlled two-thirds of the capitalist world's oil output whereas in 1982 it produced less than half. The absolute and relative decline of OPEC was the result of a combination of things: the growth of production elsewhere (such as the North Sea and the Mexican Gulf); the political turmoil in Iran followed by the Iran-Iraq war; and OPEC production cutbacks, made especially by the largest producer, Saudi Arabia, in an effort to stabilise prices at a high level. This has now become harder to do, not only because OPEC controls a smaller share of production (though it can still threaten other producers that it will flood the market), but also because the unity of the cartel itself has been breaking up. Also the advanced countries themselves have managed since the crisis to effect some reduction in their dependence on oil-produced energy; they now use 26 per cent less oil per unit of GNP than they did before the crisis.

The advanced capitalist countries did not have an unambiguously hostile attitude to the oil price increase since to some extent it was initiated by the multinational oil companies; and the US government, though it may have experienced problems as a result of the crisis, also found some of its most reactionary allies (King Khaled, and the ill-fated Shah) apparently strengthened against more left-wing currents.

In addition, the oil price increase partly resulted from the growing rivalry between the imperialist countries – some, like the USA and some minor powers like Britain and Norway expected to benefit while others like Japan and West Germany were expected to lose because they import all their oil. Also some industrialised countries expected to gain more than others from the upsurge of OPEC's demand for industrial imports. Hence the imperialist countries were far from united about the need to oppose the price increases.

The major oil companies and their role in the economy have been in many ways transformed by the oil crisis. They have been far and away the most profitable capitalist firms. The redistribution of surplus value produced by the high monopoly price of oil in a situation of profitability crisis elsewhere has contributed simultaneously to increasing the rate of profit in oil companies and lowering it further in other industries.

The combined annual turnover of the top 12 oil companies added together now amounts to 5 per cent of the total value of the world's production. The result is that they have had the resources to buy up other companies and also to enter production of other commodities on their own account. They have also had strong incentives to diversify their activities in this way since they are primarily involved in the exploitation of a wasting asset.

The oil price increase also had the effect of shattering the economic arrangements of Comecon (the economic bloc of 'socialist' countries headed by the USSR) and of producing a qualitative leap in the dimensions of the debt problems of the third world, both of which will be dealt with in more detail later in this chapter.

Breakdown of the monetary system

One clear similarity between the present crisis and the events of the 1930s has been the breakdown of a structured, relatively orderly world monetary system.

The period of dominance of the dollar (the Bretton Woods system) from 1944 to 1971 was marked by relative stability in national balance of payments, at least of the major countries, and relative stability of exchange rates apart from two periods of major, but agreed, adjustment in 1949 and the mid-1960s.

The breakdown of this system was the result of two factors. First, the collapse of confidence in the US dollar as a result of the prolonged American balance of payments deficit (accentuated by the effects of the Vietnam war); and, second, profound changes in the relative competitive positions of the different capitalist economies, in particular the decline in the competitiveness of American goods.

The 1971 crisis saw, first of all, the inability of the US government to maintain the unconditional convertibility of the US dollar. It was followed, in 1973, by the complete explosion of the existing system as the adoption of floating exchange rates by all the major capitalist powers began a decade of extreme currency instability and dizzying leaps in the price of gold and other previous metals.

These exchange rate changes were partly the result of the interplay of market forces. But also they were often encouraged by government policies in an effort to change international competitiveness. In general a lower exchange rate results in higher profits to exporters and a more competitive position. So devaluation has been used during this period as a form of protection which is less subject to international regulation than tariffs or direct import controls.

Nixon's actions in 1971 were acts of economic nationalism on the part of the United States which marked the end of a long established period of relative liberalism in international economic relations. But the victory of this 'internationalism' had never been complete and definitive. By 1971 the balance of opinion had shifted considerably and important elements of the American ruling class decided that 'internationalism' had too much eroded American privilege. Since then US national interests have been much more in the forefront of the policy priorities of American administrations and the needs of world capitalism have receded more into the background. The American devaluation of 1971 and after was a national objective won at the cost of greater instability for the system as a whole. The result of this change of tactic has been an atmosphere of intensifying conflict between the USA, West Europe and Japan over exchange rates, tariffs and other forms of protection, foreign investment rules, interest rates, expansionary and deflationary national economic policies and so on.

One of the consequences of the last ten years of world monetary upheaval and changing power relations among the advanced capitalist countries is that they have polarised increasingly into three economic camps with mutually inconsistent short-term policy objectives: the USA, Japan and the West German-dominated Europe. This aspect of the crisis has become an important extra reason (in addition to the fall in profitability and the crisis of state expenditure) why a recessionary bias has been introduced into the world economy. The Italian economist Ricardo Parboni has explained this well in his book *The Dollar and Its Rivals*:

> The financially [weak] countries are unable to take any independent initiative aimed at economic recovery – through an increase in public spending, for example – because to do so would automatically run the risk of accumulating a foreign deficit that these countries either cannot or will not finance. They therefore have to await recovery initiatives from the strong countries, which have no fundamental balance of payments problems. The impasse of the crisis is therefore an impasse in the co-ordination of national economic policies. So long as Germany and Japan refrain from reflating their economies, the rest of the capitalist world, with the exception of the United States, can only continue to stagnate.

The new protectionism

In the postwar period international trade between the major capitalist powers was liberalised in very many ways, including tariff cutting and the setting up of the EEC. The development of the crisis has now led to a renewed growth of protectionist pressures. So far these have not produced a cut-throat protectionist war on the lines of what happened in 1931, when the value of world trade was cut by two-thirds in a period of two years. Protectionism has not yet on a wide scale taken the form of the traditional instruments of tariff protection and the imposition of import controls. Instead, all kinds of ingenious disguised forms of protection have developed. In addition to competitive devaluations these have included 'buy national' campaigns, the discriminatory provision of credit, the imposition of national technical standards, 'voluntary export restraint' and so on.

Japan has maintained a more traditional protectionist policy while the USA has resorted a great deal to the enforcement of 'voluntary' restraint by foreign exporters: the EEC has been the pioneer in using technical standards on a wide scale as a protectionist measure, in addition to maintaining one of the most protectionist structures the world has ever known – the Common Agricultural Policy.

As the crisis sharpens so the intensification of national economic rivalries has grown and so, therefore, have protectionist measures. Many economists today fear that the world is poised on the brink of an abyss of protectionism. In mid-1982 a descent into tariff war between the USA and Europe over steel exports was only just averted. And Japan in particular is under constant threat of suffering measures against its exports. At present about one-fifth of them are nominally subject to measures of 'voluntary' restraint.

There has also been a growing tendency for trade restriction to be used as a punitive instrument of foreign policy. This was done by Britain and its supporters during its war against Argentina. But, more importantly, it has become a major weapon in the cold-war policy of the Reagan administration. The bans imposed against European companies supplying the Siberian pipeline were an example of the way in which the growth of inter-capitalist rivalry spills over into relations with the non-capitalist states. In this case American export bans were a disguised form of protection of US industry (by damaging their European competitors) just as, ironically, the promotion of American wheat exports to the USSR is a disguised form of protection of American agriculture.

It is just as difficult to predict whether the world will slide again into an uncontrollable trade war as it is to predict whether there will be a major financial crash. All that can be said for sure is that such an event has been a possibility for over a decade; and it looks less unlikely today than at any time before. And if it were to happen its effects on world trade could be more devastating than in the 1930s simply because world trade today is a higher proportion of total world production than it was then.

From growth to stagnation

The most notable statistical feature of the postwar boom was the constant year-after-year growth in production of goods and services in virtually all the advanced capitalist countries. That steady and consistent growth began to falter in the late 1960s. Since then economic growth has on average been much slower; it has been more erratic and fluctuations have been more uniform among countries; and actual declines in output have ceased to be rare occurrences. Recessions in other words have become deeper, longer lasting, more frequent, and more synchronised internationally. In the advanced capitalist countries growth of Gross National Product in the 1950s and 1960s averaged around 6 per cent. From 1967 to 1980 it was down to about 3 per cent.

All countries were affected by this slump. In Western Europe and the USA it is a common myth that Japan has been immune. But that is far from true. It has retained its relative advantage over other nations; but the deterioration in its economic growth has relatively speaking been even greater. From

1973 to 1980 American and European growth was one-half of its rate in the early 1960s, while in Japan growth was down to one-third of its earlier rate.

In the advanced capitalist countries as a whole the decline in the growth of investment (the guarantee of future production growth) was even more striking than the fall in production. From 1960 to 1973, it grew at 6 per cent a year or a little above. Since 1973 its annual average growth has been less than 1 per cent. Of course, an overall decline in production or fall in growth is not occurring everywhere or in all industries. There are boom industries today, like electronics, just as there were in previous economic slumps. A country like Japan, despite the end of its economic miracle, is still the envy of other capitalist countries. Even the recession-prone United States is in some way the combination of two different economies. One is the relatively booming economy of the 'sunbelt' states of the South and South-west, into which capital has been pouring in search of cheaper, non-unionised labour and a political atmosphere which imposes fewer controls on its ability to pollute the physical environment. These states have done much better than the national average in terms of growth and unemployment. And so the states of the 'frostbelt', the region of traditional industrialisation, have done correspondingly worse. It is not surprising therefore that it is generally in the big, long-industrialised, northern cities that the economic and social problems of American capitalism are most acute.

Along with production and investment world trade had also slumped. From 1970 to 1979 world merchandise trade still expanded by nearly 6 per cent a year (compared with over 8 per cent in the boom years); in 1980 that fell to 1.5 per cent and in 1981 to zero. For the advanced capitalist countries exports in 1981 grew by a mere 2 per cent.

Profits and unemployment

Unemployment expresses the central contradictions of the capitalist economy in their most naked form. In the first place, it exposes how capitalist production takes place not because of the usefulness of the goods and services which it produces – not because of the social need for them – but rather because they can be produced and sold at a profit for the capitalists.

Unemployed workers reveal that the economy has the power to produce many more useful things than are being produced. The reason that the surplus labour time and skills are not used, in spite of the pressing nature of so many social needs, is that it is not profitable for the capitalists to employ them. Yet at the same time profit in the capitalist economy only results from the employment of workers. The basis of capitalist profit is that capitalists are able to purchase the labouring ability of the workers (labour power) for wages.

The use to the capitalist of this labour power is that, unique among all commodities, it can create more value than it itself contains. This surplus value is the one and only source of profit as explained earlier in this and the previous chapter. So the existence of mass unemployment, at a time when capitalists universally complain of their failure to make adequate profits, produces a mystery: if profit comes only from the employment of wage labour, why do capitalists not employ all the unemployed workers to make profit?

Part of the answer is that profit never results *automatically* from the employment of wage labour. Many conditions have to be fulfilled: the productivity of the labour must be high enough, its wages low enough, the market demand for the product sufficient to allow the profit to be made. All these conditions must be fulfilled *simultaneously* for profits to be made. And when they are not simultaneously fulfilled for capitalists in general then the system finds itself in crisis – as today.

For the capitalists, the conditions for making profits must be re-established once again. And that means that labour during the crisis becomes not just a source of surplus value for a blood-sucking capitalist class – but also a liability. In order to establish the basis of profitability again, labour, the source of all profit, is *not* employed; it is *sacked*, *expelled* from the production process.

Marx argued that capitalism needed what he called a 'reserve army of labour' – first, to provide the opportunity to expand the most profitable areas of production without causing too many problems to existing activities; and second, in order to regulate wages and force workers in employment to work hard for fear of losing their jobs to the unemployed. Marx also argued that capitalism had a continuous tendency to recreate this reserve army by adopting new, more productive techniques and throwing redundant workers out of work. If this process did not happen rapidly enough, he believed, then the system would be thrown into crisis and for a time a new mass reserve army would suddenly be created through a slump.

Most recent events suggest that Marx's view remains basically valid today even though in so many ways the workings of the capitalist economy have changed.

The new mass unemployment

In all capitalist countries today falling profitability is leading to mass unemployment in five ways.

First, there has been a steep decline in the growth of investment in new machines and factories; and so jobs are being created by the private sector at a declining rate.

Second, some capitalists are investing in new, more productive techniques which require less labour to operate them in order to try to improve the profits of their companies. This process is inherent in capitalism at all times and rapid technological progress alone cannot lead to unemployment except of a temporary kind. It is only when it takes place in some areas of the economy while the economy as a whole does not expand fast enough to re-employ the displaced workers that it contributes to the creation of long-term unemployment. In fact the years of rising unemployment have been years of slowdown not acceleration of overall productivity growth showing that any effect of introducing new technology has been counterbalanced by the effect of the slump on reducing the efficiency of the use of machines and factories, and by other negative effects on productivity.

Third, capitalists who in periods of falling profits cannot afford to invest in new techniques and stick to the old are equally responsible for throwing more workers on to the labour market. Straining desperately to maintain their profitability they force workers to work at the greatest possible intensity and sack any who are not 'necessary'. This ruthless process goes under titles like 'rationalisation' or 'reducing overmanning', and, of course, such firms also severely cut down the rate at which they hire new workers.

Fourth, some of the firms do not make it. They are forced to close down altogether and go into liquidation or at least to shed a part of their operations and carry out factory closures. In Britain in the early 1980s redundancies were running at around 1,000 a day. This aspect of the slump in production is most acute in Britain but is affecting nearly all the major capitalist countries. Finally, there is a less direct impact of falling profits on unemployment. It is the result of spending cuts, instituted partly in order to allow the government to ease the financial situation of at least the strongest sections of capital and so help capital as a whole back to profitability.

All these developments are leading suddenly to a drop in jobs available for a growing labour force. For a decade and more there has been a dramatic fall in the number of jobs in industry, especially the manufacturing industries which have been the historical begetters of the working class. Until very recently this decline was offset by an increase in the number of jobs in the service industries, including the state sector. Now in many countries these jobs, too, are being cut back by government austerity policies. So, the decline of industrial jobs continues without any compensating employment elsewhere and the result is the present upsurge of mass unemployment.

Between eight and nine of every hundred workers in the main capitalist countries are officially unemployed. That adds up to more than 27 million workers. The OECD projected in the summer of 1982 that by 1983 the number out of work in the advanced capitalist countries would rise to 32 million.

In 1983 there will probably be at least 10 million unemployed Americans, 3½ million unemployed Britons, over 2 million each of unemployed French, West Germans and Spaniards and over half-a-million Dutch, not to mention the hundreds of millions in the third world where for obvious reasons unemployment figures are not usually published.

Unemployment was not one of the early symptoms of the crisis. For many years of falling profitability it was held in check. When the checks were removed during the 1973–75 depression the effect was like a dam bursting. The speed of increase has been frightening. The average rate of unemployment is now well over twice what it was in the closing years of the postwar boom in the main capitalist countries.

In some countries unemployment has grown much faster than in others. In France it has tripled, in Britain and Germany quadrupled, and in Spain it has increased more than six times in the space of a decade. These large differences in the recent rate of growth of unemployment between the major countries mostly result not from different rates of growth of the labour force but from different rates of creation of new jobs. Between 1974 and 1980 employment increased by 16 per cent in Canada, 13 per cent in the USA and around 6 per cent in countries such as Japan, Italy, Australia and Sweden. This helped to hold down the rate of unemployment in those countries a bit.

But in Belgium and France employment did not increase at all during those years so unemployment increased at the same rate as workers coming into the labour force. And in West Germany and Britain employment actually fell.

In most capitalist countries the rate of increase of unemployment accelerated in 1981 and 1982. And the faster the number grows the more the official figures underestimate the real numbers involved.

One major reason for the underestimation is that as unemployment grows married wormen and others who are not entitled to receive unemployment benefit do not bother to register as unemployed. In some countries, therefore, they don't appear in the official statistics, though they are no less unemployed for that. Even according to government officials, the nominal unemployment figures should be boosted by 30 per cent in the main capitalist countries to take account of this one fact alone.

Especially in some of the countries which have the lowest

unemployment figures there is another very important reason
for underestimation. It is the existence of millions of workers
on temporary contracts from countries such as Yugoslavia,
Turkey, Portugal, Spain and Algeria. In countries such as
France and Germany, the burden of unemployment has fallen
in the first instance on these 'guest workers'. Instead of signing
on and appearing in the official unemployment statistics, they
are put on trains back to their own countries to swell the
unemployment figures there. This is one of the reasons why
registered unemployment has risen so very rapidly in such
countries as Spain and Portugal.

Another reason why the unemployment figures understate
the depth of the problems of capitalism is the existence of
increasing millions of workers on short time which is a sort of
disguised form of unemployment. At present, in Britain for
example, the official figures show about 4 per cent of the labour
force on short time, which brings the total of fully and partly
unemployed to over 18 per cent of the labour force.

Finally the unemployment figures understate the problem
because most of the main capitalist countries have taken measures such as increasing the school leaving age, or setting up
'youth opportunities programmes' in the absence of which
unemployment would be even higher than it is today. Such
schemes as these do not create useful permanent job opportunities. Either they postpone briefly the time at which young
people find themselves unemployed or they simply subsidise
employers to provide jobs which they would for the most part
have provided anyway. But they do tend to create a new group
of workers employed at less than union rates and with less than
normal rights. Virtually all the governments which finance
youth employment schemes with one hand are engaged in
creating with the other hand the unemployment which makes
the schemes politically necessary.

The unequal burden

A single average figure for national unemployment can be a
very bad guide to the exact form which it is taking and the

social and political effects which it has. The first thing that the national averages conceal is differences in regional levels of unemployment. In Britain, the south-east, despite its rapid increase in unemployment, still has an overall unemployment rate only a little over half the national average, whereas in Northern Ireland there are towns and districts where the unemployment figure is over 50 per cent – and those are, of course, predominantly Catholic areas. Obviously the political implications of unemployment which is concentrated in this way are different from the same overall level of unemployment more evenly spread.

The jobless situation in Northern Ireland illustrates a principle which applies in different ways throughout the capitalist world – that it is the sections of the population which are most socially disadvantaged and powerless in the first place who suffer disproportionately from unemployment.

This applies universally in the case of women. Here is one case where the current evolution of the capitalist economies is very different from what was often predicted by Marx in the nineteenth century. He saw the capitalists' pursuit of profit leading increasingly, with the mechanisation of production tasks, to the employment of women and children – at lower wage levels – at the expense of adult male workers who would become the main element of the reserve army of labour. That is indeed what did happen in many periods of nineteenth-century capitalist development.

Today, however, as the economic crisis of capitalism leads to more unemployment it is in many places women and youth who are either thrown out of work first or who never have the chance to get a job in the first place.

The effect of the growth of women's unemployment is not only to reduce the incomes and standard of living of them and their families, if they are members of families, but also to force women out of productive social employment back into the isolation and dependence of the home and family, often into demoralisation and personal oppression.

Another section of the population universally hit in a disproportionate way by the present growth of mass unemployment is ethnic minorities. And probably the clearest case of this is the USA. While the average rate of unemployment there rose in 1982 to about 10 per cent (a little more than the international capitalist average), the rate for black Americans was over 18 per cent; and among urban blacks in cities like Detroit and Miami it is vastly greater than this – in many cases 25 per cent and beyond.

Breaking down the average even further, the levels of unemployment among black urban *youth* in the USA are commonly well in excess of 75 per cent. In 1977 the national average for teenage non-whites was 36 per cent and by August 1981 it had risen to just over 50 per cent for the whole USA. In Britain the difference between white and black unemployment levels is similar to that in the USA. In the Netherlands the overall jobless rate is 10 per cent; but for Moluccans, Surinamers and other immigrants it is 20 per cent.

The universal nature of the economic oppression of youth in the present capitalist crisis is shown by the fact that almost everywhere the rate of youth unemployment (age 15 to 24) is at least twice as high as the national average. And the problem of youth unemployment is growing more rapidly than unemployment in general. In whole countries such as Italy and Spain, and in many areas of other countries, youth unemployment is now so high that it constitutes a major social crisis by itself.

As always it is possible to break down these figures even further to show the way in which, even among youth, unemployment has a disproportionate effect on some groups. The difference between male and female unemployment is one of the most striking. In every country for which figures are available, teenage women are considerably worse hit than teenage men. In France, for example, in 1979, 14 out of every 100 male teenagers were unemployed; but the figure for women was 42 per cent.

To summarise all the complex statistics it could be said that for each worker in the capitalist countries there is about a one in twelve chance that she or he is unemployed. But for a young black woman, a member of an ethnic minority, living in an economically backward or deprived area, the chances of getting a job of any kind have been reduced in the last few years to virtually zero.

Recent figures for the United States tell this story in a vivid way; if you are a woman then, other things being equal, your chances of being unemployed are 70 per cent higher than if you are a man; if you are black the chances are 100 per cent higher than if you are white; if you are a teenager the chances are about 200 per cent higher than if you are an adult. And, adding up disadvantages, then if you are a black teenage woman your chances of being unemployed are at least 12 times as high as if you are an adult white man.

In Britain the story is just as bad. In Southwark and Brixton in South London, black unemployment is estimated at 40 per cent while black youth unemployment is said to be 80 per cent. It seems almost certain that the unemployment rate for black female teenagers must verge on 100 per cent. In Toxteth in Liverpool the overall rate of unemployment is said to be 40 per cent and that for youth 80 per cent.

It is worth noting that this phenomenon is historically unprecedented. It was not a feature of the mass unemployment of the 1930s. In fact in Britain the rates of youth unemployment then were *lower* then those for older workers. One of the reasons for this was that with less widespread unionisation it was more possible for employers to save money by firing their older workers and taking on teenagers to do the same work for less pay. Also rules on seniority (first in, last out) may not have been so strict.

For the capitalist system in general this also had the advantage that even in conditions of extreme slump some kind of viable future could be held out to a sizeable proportion of the new generation of workers. Today that is becoming well-nigh impossible. And that stark fact undermines the ability of the capitalist system to reproduce its ideological justification in the minds of the young.

The political impact of unemployment

In an effort to regain some ground on the ideological front, ruling classes throughout the world are now conducting a massive propaganda campaign alleging that it is the greed of the working class itself which creates unemployment. Workers, by demanding too much pay, or refusing to take cuts in pay, are, so the argument goes, 'pricing themselves out of a job'.

Like other notions which are propagated by bourgeois ideologists, this one has some power because it is subscribed to also by a large proportion of the established leadership of the working class. And that is possible because this notion, like others in bourgeois ideology, contains a tiny, partial element of truth.

It is true that the life of one capitalist factory, threatened with imminent bankruptcy and closure, might in some cases be extended for a time if the workers were forced to take a wage cut so that at existing prices the firm could continue to compete and make a profit. There are recent cases where workers have been 'persuaded' by this plausible-looking argument.

But the element of truth in this argument is so partial and one-sided that in reality the argument is basically false. Measures which might temporarily help the workers of a single capitalist in alliance with their exploiter, cannot, if generalised, help the working class as a whole against their exploiters.

Quite the contrary: general wage cuts under capitalism will not only fail to eliminate unemployment; they will also contribute to the creation of unemployment and the intensification of the slump. This again is a concrete illustration of the contradiction which Marx emphasised between the production and realisation of surplus value, which was discussed earlier.

The political impact of today's unemployment is very complex. Traditionally unemployment – what Marx called reconstituting the reserve army of labour – has had the effect of taming the working class by reducing its bargaining power. This is one of its effects again today and that is proved by a declining level of wage settlements in many capitalist countries in the early 1980s and in the USA the renegotiation of many labour contracts before their expiry.

But there is also today a contrary effect. The ideology of Keynesianism and the political consensus which were nurtured by the postwar boom were partly based on the idea that mass unemployment was no longer necessary or acceptable in modern capitalist society. That deeply-rooted idea, along with the growth of trade unionism, has meant that the traditional impact of mass unemployment has been reduced or delayed.

In an age when governments are held to be more responsible for the health of the economy, politics no longer follows so closely the laws of supply and demand. The new mass unemployment, therefore, is sometimes the opposite of a drag on working-class militancy: it can be a spur to political action. Furthermore, the political impact of this unemployment is different from that in earlier periods because it disproportionately affects those sections of the population who are especially likely to be militant like youth, or sections like women and ethnic minorities whose political consciousness and organisation have developed very dramatically in the last three decades.

These political contradictions mean that the question of what to pay the unemployed has become a very thorny one for capitalist governments. Many right-wing governments would still prefer to spend money on unemployment benefit rather than the same, or very little more, money on creating jobs so as to maintain the disciplinary impact of unemployment. But its continuance makes it difficult to fulfil plans for cutting government spending in slump conditions; and its continuance also reduces the effectiveness of the reserve army of labour as a drag on the bargaining power of organised labour as a whole compared with a situation where the jobless get no pay at all.

Capitalist governments are therefore seeking ways of drastically cutting back unemployment and related social security benefits. But by doing so they can only exacerbate the other – political – contradiction of their policy. That is the danger that the existence of millions of unemployed workers driven to despair and near starvation will provoke a political reaction which will threaten the stability not only of governments like Thatcher's and Reagan's but of the system which it is their overwhelming aim to rescue. A whole generation of new workers is now coming to realise that capitalism has no future to offer it.

The experience of mass unemployment in the 1930s should, however, furnish a lesson that an anti-capitalist response is not necessarily a progressive response. The fascists recruited many to their cause by railing against capitalism and its failure to provide livelihoods. The danger of a reactionary response may be all the greater when a rising proportion of the unemployed (the youth) have never belonged to organisations of labour movement self-defence such as trade unions for the simple reason that they have never had a job. It is a challenge to the labour movement to dispel that danger by recruiting the unemployed to its ranks.

The fiscal crisis of the state

While the boom years led to a steady increase in state expenditure in the major capitalist countries, the onset of the crisis suddenly accelerated that trend to the point where the burden of state spending became a specific major crisis for the system.

The main reasons for this are the decline in profits in both private and nationalised industries which have led governments, afraid of massive industrial collapse, to bail out industries facing financial crisis. But the bankruptcies and cutbacks which have occurred as part of the same process have led to a huge increase in the need for social payments – unemployment benefit in particular – far beyond what was ever foreseen when unemployment insurance became universal in the advanced countries.

In addition the failure to foresee the rapid rate of inflation to which the crisis gave rise has also made government expenditures career out of control and has helped to create what has been called by James O'Connor in his important and prophetic book, a 'fiscal crisis of the state'.

At the start of the crisis O'Connor predicted that the kinds of state spending which would rise most rapidly were those needed to stabilise the capitalist system (like propaganda and repression) rather than those devoted to directly productive purposes related to capital accumulation. It is difficult to verify whether this is what has actually taken place. But his other predictions of rising state expenditures as a share of national income and of increasing difficulties in financing this spending have certainly been realised.

Due to the effects of the crisis, revenues in advanced capitalist countries have failed to keep pace with spending. During the postwar boom capitalist countries, taking one year with another, did not run government deficits. The old accumulated state debt (largely from the war years) was steadily devalued by inflation. But as the crisis developed government deficits became more and more general as state expenditure came to have more weight in the economy.

In 1960 state spending was 28.4 per cent of the national income of the OECD countries; and tax receipts were more or less in line with this at 28.3 per cent. By 1978 spending had risen to 38.2 per cent of national income while receipts had risen only to 35 per cent. The OECD's latest estimates for all the advanced countries are that these deficits will creep up to around 4 per cent of GNP for 1982 and 1983 despite almost universal austerity policies.

The commitment of numerous governments to combat creeping deficits has proved to be extremely difficult to keep. This may partly be the result of what economists call 'built-in stabilisers'. When there is an economic downturn tax receipts tend to be lower because sales and incomes are lower; and spending tends to be higher because more people qualify for 'entitlement state benefits' like unemployment pay or income supplement. The stabilisers have not been nearly as effective as some Keynesians once predicted. But without them unemployment in the 1970s would almost certainly have grown even faster than it did.

The stabilisers mean that governments who aim to balance their budget in recessionary times have a tough job. They deny that high state spending is an elixir of youth and complain that it is toxic to the system. But they have failed to realise that it has become an addictive drug for capitalist economies. Withholding it can cause serious withdrawal symptoms; and worse than that the system's tolerance for the drug appears to be growing and so, to carry on functioning, it needs bigger and bigger fixes.

In practice so far, although finance is a major question for *national* states their control over the printing of money means that it has not reached catastrophic proportions. The fiscal crisis of the state, especially in Britain, the USA and Italy, has become particularly acute at the level of *municipalities*.

This is for three reasons: that is where many of the most demanding social spending programmes are concentrated; the municipalities receive most of their finance from the central state which can therefore cut off their funds; and municipalities have no power to print money, limited powers to borrow independently of central government and little ability to impose local taxes or raise their own revenue in other ways. On the other hand local authority spending has risen faster than central government spending. In Britain, for example, local authority spending rose from under 10 per cent to about 20 per cent of national income from 1950 to 1980.

In Britain a long and bitter war has been taking place between the central government under Thatcher and many municipalities in the government's fight to cut public expenditure and force a cutback in social provision and staff redundancies on local authorities. The same is beginning to happen in the United States as a result of Reagan's attempts to cut the US budget while raising defence spending.

In Britain, routine and then punitive cutbacks in central government funding (which finances about 50 per cent of local authority spending) have been met by local authorities with various combinations of rate increases, supplementary rate impositions and cuts in real expenditure. The problem has now, however, reached such massive proportions that solutions of this kind may not be possible within the time span permitted by the government. The result may be city bankruptcies, wholesale closing of social services and equivalent sacking of staff with possible major political confrontations as a result.

In the USA, too, the pressure is on local (state and city) governments since many of Ronald Reagan's Federal government cutbacks have been effected simply by sloughing responsibilities off on to the local governments without providing them with any new sources of revenue.

Profits and inflation

The rise of inflation is in some ways the most visible element in the change from boom to crisis since we all encounter it every time we go shopping.

The two postwar decades in the main capitalist countries were ones for the most part of slow and steady inflation. But in the late 1960s and the 1970s average rates of inflation suddenly jumped up. In some cases (in Britain and Italy, for instance) they seemed for a time to threaten currency stability in a serious way. As the 1970s wore on these extreme rates came more under control. But the capitalist world as a whole seemed destined to continue at a historically high inflation rate of around 10 per cent in spite of very strong deflationary measures being taken by governments.

The rate of inflation is one important link in the circular chain of relationships between profits, wages, productivity, prices and the money supply. In modern industrial capitalist economies prices usually do not move automatically according to fluctuations of demand and supply in a free market. Though prices may respond to changes in supply and demand they are mostly fixed by a decision of producers or distributors.

Two main elements enter into their decision. A price must be low enough to ensure there is sufficient demand for the amount of the product the producer needs to sell. But also a price must be high enough to cover costs of production and make the desired profit for the capitalist. This contradiction which faces every capitalist producer is yet another instance of the problems of simultaneously producing and realising surplus value.

Capitalists have tended to put up their prices more rapidly in the last decade in order to compensate for the erosion of their profits through rising costs. In many instances they have even become prepared to sacrifice some of their market to ensure that they produce a more limited output at a profit. Profit margins have themselves been eroded by rising costs, sometimes from imported goods such as oil, sometimes from wages or from other sources.

The essence of inflation, therefore, is that it is the manifestation of a conflict over the distribution of income. Workers and consumers must battle to prevent inflation from cutting their living standards and that means fighting for increases in money wages and in state and other financial benefits. Capitalists retaliate by raising prices again. Inflation is not in this way a consequence of any one single cause. It is part of a complex causal chain.

The fact that inflation is higher in the crisis than it was in the boom reflects the fact that falling profitability has made the struggle over distribution a much sharper one – it is sharper both between capital and labour and between different sections of capital and different nations of the capitalist world. Just as inflation has been a weapon of the capitalists in the class struggle so it is also a weapon of the oil producing countries in gaining a larger share of the world's surplus value. But it makes no sense to blame inflation on a single cause like OPEC's greed or 'excessive' wage demands by workers.

Because inflation is something which seems to be simultaneously and uniformly bad for all social groups, capitalist governments have tried to argue with some success that it is a national problem whose causes must be tackled for the potential benefit of all.

On closer examination, however, this argument appears to be rather defective. It is true that some aspects of inflation harm capitalists. It can erode competitive advantages in relation to the capitalists of other countries and so reduce profits; it always threatens to accelerate and so increase financial uncertainty; and financial instability is usually bad for production and investment. And for workers inflation quite simply erodes the value of their wages whatever they may be. But inflation does not have equally bad effects on all social classes because its speed relative to the growth of wages and productivity affects the distribution of income between wages and profits. If wages rise faster than prices and productivity combined then capitalists can find their share of the national income falling in the process of inflation. It is this fact rather than the fact of inflation itself which has alarmed capitalists in much of the postwar period.

Hence 'remedies' for inflation usually take the form of reducing the standard of living of workers through wage restrictions, cuts in government spending and monetary squeezes, because they are really remedies for falling profitability (a much more politically indecent form of words). But even in periods when the capitalists are gaining from the inflationary spiral they worry about inflation because it tends to excite hostility to the system which gives birth to it. So capitalists, though they use inflation, tend to oppose it both for its own sake and because it has been built by their own propaganda into a general anathema. Hence policies designed to attack workers' material interests by more direct means than inflation come under the disguise of a national struggle against inflation, allegedly the alien enemy of all.

So far, laborious efforts to reduce inflation in the advanced countries have failed to bring it down much below 10 per cent on average. It is beginning to be recognised that the consequences of bringing down the increase of prices are so severe (especially in terms of unemployment and decimated social services) that the cure produces as many political problems as the disease.

Yet a return to expansionism and higher inflation is still regarded as a worse evil because it is not expected to solve the basic problem of profitability. Once again this is an example of the gigantic problem of restoring the shattered equilibrium of the capitalist system. Improving one aspect of the problem stubbornly worsens another. Capitalist governments are as perplexed as Alice in Wonderland when she attempted to restore herself to a normal size by eating and drinking various magic substances: she always grew too large or too small.

Crisis in the third world

The crisis is having the effect of intensifying all the negative trends which were already visible in the underdeveloped countries during capitalism's good years. Unemployment, poverty and inequality are growing. The annual growth rate of their GNP per head seems to be steadily declining. From 1960 to 1973 it was about 3.8 per cent; it fell to 2.4 per cent from 1973 to 1979. In 1980 it was down to 1.8 per cent and in 1981 down to 0.2 per cent.

There is not the space here to show how this is affecting some 100 or so individual countries. But there is one particular question which has become a very dramatic one as a result of the crisis – that of international indebtedness – which will be looked at here in more detail.

The overall value of the debts of the underdeveloped countries has grown steadily since the war. This has largely been the result of 'economic aid' in which capitalist governments loaned money to the governments of the underdeveloped countries. Allegedly this was to finance long-term development though most often it was wasted or ended up financing bureaucrats' bank accounts in Switzerland or arms sales. Nevertheless, though used by the imperialists as a weapon of political control, it did not become a source of economic or financial crisis in the underdeveloped countries since it could always be re-scheduled by the imperialist governments and often was.

Since the early 1970s, however, the problem has changed qualitatively. In the first place the amount of debt has skyrocketed, due in particular to the sudden catastrophic deterioration in the third world's balance of payments which followed the oil price increase. The total has risen from $64 billion in 1970 to nearly $600 billion in 1982. Since their export prices have fallen significantly in this period this is a more than ten-fold real increase. Second, the type of debt has changed. State loans from the imperialist countries have relatively declined, while the bulk of the increase in debt has been to exporting firms in the form of trade credit or to banks largely in the form of short-term loans. About 65 per cent of the debt is now to private creditors, compared with 45 per cent in 1970.

This is the result of the 'happy accident' that, simultaneously with the worsening of the balance of payments position, the slump and crisis in the imperialist countries resulted in the banks having a sudden surplus of loanable funds and capitalists having unsold goods which they could only sell by urging the acceptance of deferred payments plans on their unsuspecting customers.

So the results of this process in the aggregate are: a sharp rise in indebtedness and repayment obligations compared both with the national income and the value of exports of the underdeveloped countries; a decrease in the average time over which debts have to be repaid (from 18.6 years in 1973 to 14.7 years today); a rise in the average nominal interest rate (from 6.6 to 7.9 per cent); and that means a rise in the real interest rate measured in relation to commodity prices from a negative figure in the early 1970s to over 16 per cent in 1982; a shortening of grace periods before the first repayments are due (from 5.6 years to 4.7 years); the growing possibility of forced bankruptcy and default; and an increase in the stranglehold of capitalist institutions such as the IMF and the international banks over the economies of the underdeveloped countries.

In a way these aggregate results both exaggerate and understate the problem. Some of the most indebted countries have no serious problems in paying what they owe and have deliberately borrowed very heavily against expected future revenue. This seems to apply to Brazil. On the other hand in mid-1982 most economists were still confidently saying that it also applied to Mexico which has vast oil resources not yet developed. Yet at that moment Mexico entered a colossal financial crisis partly as a result of its high international indebtedness. At the same time many of the poorest countries which have a relatively low level of indebtedness feel its effects much more heavily as the vampire's teeth sink into their necks.

One of the causes of international indebtedness has been the legendary instability of the export earnings of some underdeveloped countries. Many of them still earn foreign exchange mainly by exporting a limited number of primary products. From 1950 to 1980 primary commodity prices (except for oil) fell by one half. But during that period they have fluctuated up and down. Since the boom in prices of 1973–74 they have fallen by about 40 per cent. To give some very recent examples: between mid-1981 and mid-1982, a year of industrial recession in the advanced countries, the price of cocoa fell by 33 per cent, rubber by 30 per cent and sugar by 60 per cent. Unfortunately for the countries which produce those products the internal combustion engine does not run on cocoa, rubber or sugar.

If there is no world financial collapse indebtedness will have to continue to grow. This is because the balance of payments deficit of the underdeveloped countries is expected to be around $100 billion a year for the foreseeable future even to maintain present levels of consumption.

In many of the poorest underdeveloped countries economic conditions for the mass of the people are worsening fast. During the 1970s no less than 45 out of the 96 poorest countries experienced a decline in food production per head. Out of 38 African countries, as many as 26 produced less food per head in 1979 than they had in 1969. In fifty countries daily calorie supply was calculated to be below basic requirements.

The absolute and probably relative number of starving people in the world is growing. Yet the problems of the crisis are used as a pretext for curtailing even those very limited programmes of useful international economic aid which exist.

Crisis in the 'socialist' states

There is not enough space here to analyse fully the economic situation in the 'socialist' states of the USSR, Eastern Europe and China. But a profile of the current crisis would be incomplete if it did not at least summarise some of the increasing interrelations between the economic problems of the capitalist states and those of the bureaucratically planned economies.

The 'socialist' economies are still relatively isolated from the rest of the world economy. They tend to be more autarkic (self-sufficient) economies than any in the capitalist world. Even the USSR exports less than a small country like Belgium. And over half the international trade of Comecon countries still takes place within that group of countries.

But several things have made these countries increasingly dependent on the rest of the world, especially for imports: their need for advanced technology in fields where they have failed to develop it; shortages of strategic raw materials; the failures of USSR-style planning to supply needed goods; and the chronic crisis of Soviet agriculture.

By importing these things from the capitalist world the planned economies have been gradually sucked into the capitalist economic whirlpool and new problems have been added to those which their economies were experiencing already which have led to regular scaling down of planned rates of growth.

The rulers of these states have faced growing political problems as mass opposition has developed to their police-state dictatorships at just the moment when the capitalist world has been descending into crisis.

In these economic conditions Comecon countries have had little possibility of selling more of their relatively low quality manufactured goods to the West – and the markets they have built up in some underdeveloped countries have been badly hit by the effects of the crisis, especially by the rise in the price of oil.

So the East European bureaucracies have been forced to try to square a circle: they have needed to import more under conditions where they cannot earn the needed money by exporting more to convertible currency areas.

The answer has been – debt. Very rapidly the 'socialist' countries have contracted considerable debts to capitalist banks which have as a result gained increasing leverage in the centrally planned economies. Today, Eastern European economic planners are obliged to divulge much more information about their economies to capitalist bankers than they do to their own workers in whose name they claim to rule.

The extreme case of all this is of course Poland where the bureaucratic dictatorship has faced a simultaneous political and economic crisis. Poland since 1980 is an extreme example of many things. It exemplifies the present-day strength of the struggle of the working class, and the crisis of the productive system. It is also one of the most perilously indebted countries in the world. Its debts per head of the population are nearly the highest of any country (though less than those of Ireland or Belgium). And at the same time its negotiable international assets are virtually the lowest of any country in the world.

The Polish crisis more than anything else has led to the intertwining of the crisis of the 'socialist' and capitalist economies. Today a high-powered committee of international bankers, representing the five hundred or so banks to which Poland owes money, is in more or less permanent session considering the economic problems of Poland and the continual rescheduling of the debt payments it cannot meet. These bankers play a crucial role in the drama now being played out on the stage of Eastern Europe. By their decisions about how liberal to be about debt repayment they can make a major impact on the way the Polish crisis evolves.

If the banks are not generous about rescheduling the debt which Poland cannot pay, they will oblige the Polish rulers to try to get the money either by leaning more on the Soviet Union or by trying to squeeze the Polish workers and peasants even harder. If the reaction to that is a further development of militant anti-government action, it will please neither the directly threatened Polish rulers nor their capitalist creditors. The latter not only stand to lose the money they unwisely invested in Poland where they thought the workers had been tamed, but also to see the example of the Polish workers spreading even to the capitalist world.

Not only is there a strong link between the overall economic fate of capitalist and bureaucratic 'socialist' countries, but the conflicts *within* each of the two groups now affect the other. Capitalist nations have since the late 1960s been trying to build the economy of China so that it can be a more effective counterweight to the Soviet Union. And more recently a split has opened between the capitalist countries over how much to aid the development of the USSR. The most striking example of that was President Reagan's attempt in mid-1982 to sabotage the building of the great and potentially lucrative Siberia-Western Europe gas pipeline, whose construction would aid the economies of both the USSR and the rival West European capitalist nations (especially West Germany) in comparison with the United States.

The Soviet leaders now face a situation where the long-term development of the USSR is seen as linked with the economies of Western Europe but where their shorter-term needs for cash and wheat make them still depend on American banks and the

American government. Hence a further growth in inter-capitalist rivalry can be expected to have an even sharper impact of a complex kind on the Soviet economy.

A world of bad debts

Looming frighteningly over the deliberations of the committee of world bankers which manages Poland's debts has been the possibility of major default. This would, as everybody knows but few dare say, be a staggering blow to the stability of the world's financial system. Many bankers fear that it could be the trigger of a monumental financial crash. All the historians of the 1920s observe that one of the problems which resulted in the crash of 1929 was the overextension of credit in the world and especially in the USA. That memory haunts the world today. The growth of credit (and so indebtedness) in the post-war world has almost certainly been hundreds of times greater than it was in the 1920s. Within countries consumer credit has expanded massively through hire purchase, bank loans and mortgages. Business firms have financed a growing proportion of their investment and stock-building through bank loans. Internationally, most exports are now financed through export credit schemes. Business firms and states borrow more and more just to stay afloat.

A few years ago, it was common to dismiss out of hand the idea that this was a dangerous situation. New credit and banking institutions, it was said, were much stronger than in the 1920s and 1930s. And the big international debtors were highly creditworthy countries. It is true that some of the weaknesses which led to the widespread collapse of banks in the USA have been rectified and the capitalist world's financial system in the last three decades has become extraordinarily innovative and flexible. But whatever clever schemes can be devised for rolling over credit, or rescheduling and restructuring debts, the ugly fact remains that a bad debt is a bad debt. And the nature of debt is such that one bad debt, if it is important enough, can rapidly infect the whole system.

Within the last few years several important banks and financial companies have failed in the USA. In the aftermath of the 1974–75 recession, 27 US banks failed. In the early 1980s only action by the Federal government and the Morgan Guaranty Trust Company (one of New York's giant international banks) rescued several savings banks (including the Greenwich, the nation's third largest) from bankruptcy, and 1982 saw the collapse of the Penn Square Bank of Oklahoma, and Drysdale Government Securities. Damaging bankruptcies have also been rising in number. The years 1981 and 1982 saw companies the size of Laker and Braniff Airways, International Harvester and AEG Telefunken become bad debtors. Mortgage arrears in the USA doubled between 1979 and 1981. Dramatic flurries of financial panic followed the collapse of the Herstadt Bank in Germany in the early 1970s, and the bankruptcy of the Banco Ambrosiano in Italy in 1982.

Perhaps most seriously of all, in the early 1980s Poland was not the only nation which entered into a state of near bankruptcy. It was quickly followed by at least two of the other superdebtors, namely Argentina, after the South Atlantic war with Britain, and, more surprisingly, Mexico. These disturbing events led to a prediction by some bankers at a Bank of International Settlements meeting in 1982 that some $200 billion of official international debts were 'of dubious quality', that is potentially bad debts.

It is not often realised that by far the largest debtor nation in the world is the United States. The significance of debt for the nation which prints the world money is different from its significance for other less privileged countries. But the dollar liabilities of the US government (held both by Central Banks as reserves and in private holdings by banks, businesses and individuals) run into hundreds of billions of dollars. It is certainly not impossible that a panic speculative move against the dollar could occur. If it did the whole system of world trade and payments would suffer the consequences which would be appallingly deflationary.

All this has led some analysts to say that the tremors of the last few years are precursors of a major financial earthquake. That certainly looks less far-fetched than it did a few years ago.

At the beginning of the 1980s there was a mushroom-like expansion of the big corporate and national debtors seeking to be baled out of bad debts. It remains to be seen, if there is such a disaster, whether the financial structure has been made more earthquake-proof than in the 1930s.

Flashpoints of the crisis

It is clear that the basic economic crisis of the capitalist system has not begun to be resolved. The main symptom of it, the fall in the rate of profit, has nowhere been appreciably reversed despite the multitude of measures taken to reverse it. We cannot predict in very concrete terms what will happen economically and politically but at the economic level there is every reason to expect that most of the trends of the last few years will continue and maybe spread and intensify. These include the growth of mass unemployment, growing indebtedness at every level, the crisis of state expenditure, the cutback of state-provided social services, and the bankruptcy of capitalist firms.

The evidence of the previous pages shows that the effects of the crisis can best be seen not in the form of average statistics. Those averages are made up of some areas and groups which are not affected so severely or even do well in the crisis and others, the worse than average, which are affected that much more severely. The problem of unemployment, as well as being a general one for the whole working class, is very acutely one for the young, for blacks, for women. The political consequences of unemployment therefore will be particularly influenced by the reaction of those particularly hard-pressed groups.

Likewise the problem of state finance is also a general one but especially concentrated in municipal finance and within that especially in municipalities responsible for depressed inner-city areas in industrial cities. These are the very areas, of course, where the first problem of unemployment tends to be most acute and socially explosive. And likewise the international debt problem is concentrated in a few of the poorer countries of the world.

Social and economic explosions cannot be easily predicted. The breaking point of any social phenomenon cannot be decided in advance. Today there is a far higher proportion of inner-city youth without work than ever before in capitalist history. There is a higher ratio of credit (and therefore debt – national, state, corporate and personal) to national income than at any previous moment in history.

Many people will boldly predict that unprecedented facts of this kind – and we could all produce many more examples – will definitely result in massive political and economic upheavals in the near future. Such possibilities exist and socialists must be prepared for them as much as possible. Yet similar apocalyptic predictions have been made on numerous occasions in the last decade and have usually proved to be extremely exaggerated. There has been insufficient attempt to try to understand in a rigorous way what exactly are the limits of endurance of the capitalist system and the interrelations of politics and economics.

We can be certain that the capitalist system for all its problems and potential crises will not collapse of its own accord or wither away. We can see that it retains enormous power – economic, military and ideological. And as socialists we have to devote at least as much attention to understanding why it survives for so long as we do to identifying its problems and the way it fails to fulfil social needs.

Part of that task is to analyse, and not only denounce, the plans which the unprepared capitalist class and its political leaders are devising and implementing to cure the crisis.

5.

The Capitalist Search for a Way Out

The death of consensus

The economic crisis raises vital problems for or imposes heavy burdens on virtually all those who live in capitalist society – except maybe for a few clever or lucky profiteers who gain out of the misfortunes of others.

But different social groups see a very different content to the crisis. Most capitalists see first and foremost a decline in their rate of profit and they imagine a whole set of other things to be associated with this: wages rising 'too fast', productivity rising 'too slowly', inflation, high interest rates, high raw material prices, stagnant markets and so on. But as a whole the capitalist class has not arrived at a consistent and unified view of what the crisis consists of and why it is happening, let alone of what to do about it.

The old intellectual certainties of Keynesianism, so universally held, have been exploded altogether and the old consensus politics replaced by polarisation. The economically impossible has now happened so many times and in so many places that there is no longer *any* accepted conventional wisdom about the economy except that things are bad and will quite probably worsen before they get better.

Increasingly the bourgeoisie, politically and intellectually, is dividing into two camps. One camp, the radical right, is dominated by the threat to the overall system of profitable exploitation posed by the economic crisis. Members of that camp see the question ever more clearly in class terms and have set themselves consciously the task of undoing the economic knot tied during the boom years by arranging a fundamental redistribution of wealth and power away from working people and their families. If this involves the creation of mass unemployment and the manifest failure to meet even elementary social needs then, they say, so be it.

Virtually all capitalist governments have in the last decade made important inroads into traditional democratic freedoms. And there are growing signs in a number of countries that the kind of solutions envisaged by this section of the bourgeoisie, or even lesser austerity programmes, simply cannot be carried out in the context of parliamentary democracy and trade union freedoms. We can expect that the most determined and perspicacious sections of this part of the bourgeoisie will act on the consequences and move, perhaps in alliance with the erratically growing fascists, towards more authoritarian solutions.

Another section of the bourgeoisie, though not at present imbued with such political prestige or influence, are in Britain referred to as the 'wets', a male-chauvinist term coined by those to their right. The 'wets' recoil in horror at the extreme consequences of the measures which the radical right tell them are necessary to preserve the capitalist system which they support. Intellectually they represent the remains of Keynesianism. They are to be found both in the 'left' of capitalist parties and in the reformist workers' parties such as the British Labour Party, the French and Spanish Socialist Parties, the German Social Democrats and the 'Eurocommunist' Parties. Though they support more state spending to preserve employment, and more economic aid to combat world poverty, they do not represent a radical current. They are for the most part clinging to old, used policies which have lost prestige because they have been seen to fail. Often, therefore, their hopes, like those of less closeted lovers of the free market, are placed on some semi-automatic upturn in the economy.

The failure of governments in capitalist countries to unite on a strategy to deal with the crisis partly reflects the fact that there are objective differences of interest between distinct sections of the capitalist class. There seems to be no set of economic policies from which all sections of capital can benefit.

A marxist analysis of the crisis helps us to understand why this is so. The process of raising the rate of profit after it has fallen to unacceptable levels consists, according to marxist analysis, of raising the amount of surplus value produced and realised, or lowering the value of the total capital over which it must be shared, or some combination of the two. The important thing, as discussed earlier, is to increase surplus value *relative* to the value of capital.

This means that some sections of capital, which may be able to raise the productivity of the workforce in their employ or which may have a buoyant market for their product, will oppose policies which are designed to keep afloat those sections of capital which are not so favourably placed. From the point of view of the survival of the capitalist class the more successful sections of it may well support the idea that the crisis would be helped by the destruction or purge of the less successful portion of capital. Yet obviously those more hard-pressed sections of capital will favour policies which help them to survive, and that almost certainly means policies which, usually via the state, redistribute surplus value. Conflicts over policy within the capitalist class, then, very often centre around the question of state expenditure and the extent to which it should be curtailed.

A related source of conflict concerns the question of wages. In one sense all sections of capital will benefit if wages can be curtailed relative to productivity since, other things being equal, this will raise the rate of exploitation of the labour force. On the other hand a whole section of capital depends for its survival on producing commodities which are by and large consumed by the working class. For them any curtailment of wages, therefore, is a curtailment of the market for their products and so of their ability to realise surplus value.

Ultimately for capitalists as a whole, this is a conflict or contradiction which cannot be completely resolved. It demands a perpetual balancing act. But for sections of capital in the short run there may seem to be no contradiction at all. So the contradiction for capital as a whole gets expressed as a conflict of interest and policy between different sections of the capitalist class over state expenditure and wage control in particular.

A related dispute concerns international trade and protection. Protectionism, and the shrinkage of markets which it usually brings about, is not in the interests of capital as a whole on a world scale. Nonetheless certain sections of capital, those subjected to the hottest competition and which produce mainly for the home market, may well see protection as a perfect solution to their own immediate problems.

All these objective conflicts of economic interest are part of the cause of the differences over policy which have erupted in the capitalist class since the present crisis commenced. In addition, there are differences which are more political in nature. Even if the economic objectives could be sorted out, there would remain disagreements over how much the necessary strategy to increase the rate of profit should be imposed through head-on political conflict with the potential victims of the policies and how much those victims should be cajoled and persuaded to collaborate in their own fate.

The radical right

The break-up of the economic consensus in capitalist societies has partly been the result of the emergence of new strategies of the 'radical right' in dealing with the problems which the crisis raises before the capitalist class.

As already mentioned, one of the main differences between the old Keynesian section of the bourgeoisie and the new radical right has been over the question of state expenditure. Radical right governments have launched ambitious plans to make major reductions in state-provided services and state support for industry and other subsidies, combined usually with plans for simultaneous cuts in taxation to restore incentives in the private economy and produce a radical reversal in the tendency of modern capitalism towards greater state involvement in production.

Closely linked with this attitude towards state spending is a policy of severe control of the money supply which many right-wingers argue gets out of control and causes inflation mainly through uncontrolled state spending and debt. Though backed up with sophisticated-looking statistics, this monetarism is really no more than old-fashioned deflation.

These more traditional right-wing policies of opposition to the big state and financial conservatism have recently been joined by a new variety of right-wing economic doctrine known in America as 'supply-side economics'.

Supply-siders argue that policies affecting demand can't work. The cost of reducing inflation by cutting state demand is a degree of slump which even to them is unacceptable. The problem, they say, is to reverse the built-in tendency of the system to discourage saving and investment. And that, they argue, means increasing incentives for the potential investors, that is, the rich and the capitalists. And that, in turn, means cutting the marginal tax rates for higher incomes.

Some of them even maintain that such a policy will actually increase government tax revenue because of the stimulus it would give to economic activity. But their main point is that supply-side policies of tax reductions for the rich would benefit everybody since they are the only way in which investment, rapid growth, reindustrialisation, the return of full employment and prosperity can be restored.

Of course these supply-siders with their complete opposition to progressive taxes (i.e. higher tax rates on higher incomes) hark back to earlier right-wing traditions. As one of their American advocates, the journalist George Gilder, has proclaimed: 'Regressive taxes help the poor . . . To help the poor and middle classes one must reduce the tax rates of the rich.' A series of similar remarks could no doubt be traced back to Marie Antoinette and beyond.

Supply-siders within the capitalist class, like unreconstructed Keynesians, hold the view that recovery from the crisis can take place without basic opposition between the capitalist and the working classes. They are fond of quoting John F. Kennedy's remark that 'a rising tide lifts all boats'.

Although the supply-siders have been gaining influence, in general the purist ones are regarded as cranks even by the capitalist class. But the effect of their one-sided ideas has been to concentrate more attention within the ruling class on the problems which marxists would see as being associated with the production rather than the realisation of surplus value. In this sense they redress some of the imbalance of the traditional Keynesian approach. Their tax policies have often been combined by sections of the bourgeoisie with a more ruthless approach towards the weaker sections of capital to produce some of the new right policies which have been enunciated by the governments of Margaret Thatcher in Britain and Ronald Reagan in the USA.

But the more far-sighted sections of this new right maintain an understanding that neither Keynesianism nor supply-side economics are the magic wand they claim to be. Both of them ignore the very basic fact of class conflict within capitalist society and conceal the fact that the resolution of the crisis cannot take place with out a major shift in the balance of class forces.

Thatcher and Reagan have in common a knowledge that the implementation of their policies will require a frontal attack on the working class through unemployment, the wholesale destruction of social services and real wage cuts. In order to achieve these it will probably be necessary for big fights to take place between the employers and government on the one hand and trade unions on the other.

A realisation of what is necessary, however, does not mean that it can be easily achieved, as a look at the chequered careers of Thatcherism and Reaganomics shows.

Thatcherism

In Britain the landslide election victory of Margaret Thatcher's radical right government in 1979 has been described by its chief economic minister Geoffrey Howe as being like the arrival of the US cavalry in a Hollywood western. Initially, indeed, the Thatcher government seemed to be a new authoritative beacon for the bourgeoisie on a world scale; yet by early 1982 it was fighting for its political life with virtually all of its once shining economic policies badly tarnished. It was only able to quench the fires of public discontent by directing at them a hose of chauvinist propaganda and waging war against Argentina. For a time economic opposition to Thatcher could virtually be branded as pro-Argentinian treason. Thatcher's political come-back in mid-1982 certainly had nothing to do with economic success.

The problems of Thatcherism have partly been economic ones in the narrow sense. Efforts to cut the money supply have failed because a good portion of the monetary system is not effectively within the control of the state monetary authorities. Second, efforts to cut government spending and the state sector deficit have failed because what the policies cut from state spending by the ending of health, education and other services, they add on in the form of unemployment and social security benefits. A parliamentary Select Committee recently estimated that in Britain the cost to the state of the present level of unemployment was £15 billion a year – one and a half times the size of the government deficit.

The sharpness of this problem was not quite foreseen by the Thatcher government. Certainly they intended to create mass unemployment but they probably did not envisage that this would be on the scale that has in fact occurred. That, perhaps, more than anything else, has led to the rapid political disillu-sionment with the Thatcher government. And the fear of the political consequences for its survival has led a section of the government itself to be increasingly openly hostile to full-blooded Thatcherism and have also led to important retreats by the more hardcore Thatcherites themselves. When Minister of Industry, Keith Joseph, continued financial aid to various loss-making nationalised and private industries which should, according to his own criteria, have gone bankrupt and piled even more workers onto the unemployment scrapheap.

In addition, the experiences of Thatcher and now Reagan are revealing another problem with the monetarist aspect of their strategy – that it is almost bound to lead to international divisions within the ranks of the capitalist countries. Recent economic summits at Ottawa in 1981 and Versailles in 1982 found all the other capital countries, including Britain, putting pressure on Ronald Reagan to take steps to reduce interest rates in the USA and so reduce the pressure that high American interest rates pile on their own economies. Monetarism has turned out to be necessarily monetarism in one country. Like Keynesianism and protectionism it turns out to be a policy which may do something to alleviate the economic problems of one capitalist nation but only at the cost of worsening those of others.

The bold experiment of Thatcherism then has fallen far short of its objectives. So far it looks as if Reaganomics is not going to fare any better.

Reaganomics – an inconsistent experiment

Compared with its immediate predecessors, Reaganomics is a radical new attempt to solve the problems of capitalist crisis, clearly in the interests of the capitalist class.

Radical and new it may be – but intellectually coherent it is not. In fact, the Reagan administration consists of an alliance, or perhaps more appropriately a scrambled mish-mash, of several economic ideas. First there are the budget balancers, led until recently by Reagan himself. Their main economic objective in the period up to 1984 is, or rather was, the complete elimination of the budget deficit. Given that Reagan was elected on a grandiose promise to cut taxes by 30 per cent during his term of office and at the same time to vastly increase military spending, this means that the policy of cutting the deficit implies huge cuts in government spending on virtually everything other than the military.

Reagan's chief lieutenant in his programme of ruthless cuts has been David Stockman, a young former Congressman, appointed by Reagan as Director of the Office of Management and the Budget. From the OMB, Stockman has since 1980 conducted an obsessional drive against every aspect of government spending. The emphasis of this drive has been against what have been euphemistically termed 'non-essential services' (that is, anything which directly affects the welfare of disadvantaged citizens). The consequences of this first major dose of

Reaganomics, as of Thatcherism, is that those in society who was disadvantaged to begin with are relatively the worst hit, because they have relied most on the government programmes established during the boom.

Reagan's cuts campaign reach its *reductio ad absurdum* when such proposals were seriously made as the redefinition of tomato ketchup as a vegetable so that the cost of school meals could be reduced while meeting statutory nutritional standards. Public ridicule, and opposition even by a leading member of the Heinz family to the elevation of ketchup, led to the withdrawal of this proposal. But the cutbacks have meant the removal or reduction in availability of food stamps and of medical aid to several million needy Americans. And the real value of many state benefits were reduced during the first two years of Reagan's administration.

But the budget deficit was not cut. At first it went on soaring out of control with each successive estimate. This did not greatly worry the second element of the Reaganomics coalition – the supply-siders. In spite of their general opposition to spending cuts, the supply-siders have seen one of their best selling books, George Gilder's *Wealth and Poverty*, praised by David Stockman as 'Promethean in its intellectual power and insight' and journalist Gilder at once returned the compliment.

In *Wealth and Poverty* he endorses the economic theories of an obscure Southern Californian Professor of Business named Arthur Laffer (whose 'Laffer curve' allegedly proves that tax cuts increase government revenue), and endorses the similar ideas of *Wall Street Journal* editor Jude Wanniski, author of *The Way the World Works*. Of the latter work, Laffer has said, 'In all honesty, I believe it is the best book on economics every written'. Just as they insist that capitalists thrive on unfettered opportunities to make profit, supply-siders themselves appear to thrive on adulation (most of it mutual).

These intellectual (for want of a better word) high priests of the supply side say that for capital to recover, all assistance must be given to the present and potential entrepreneurs. That means (they say) allowing capitalist investors to pocket more of their earnings – and so, more than anything, reducing taxes, especially on profits and any other form of capitalist income.

The tax cuts introduced under Reagan will make very little difference to the real take-home pay of lower and middle-paid workers. All that can be said is that without the tax cuts, the amount they pay in taxes would have tended to go up. And in 1982 the administration changed tack on the tax question by forcing through Congress an Act which would raise taxes by $100 billion a year by means of what were euphemistically called 'measures of revenue enhancement'. (If Nixon's was the administration of expletives, Reagan's is the administration of euphemisms.)

Tax cuts were never very popular with the third element in the Reaganomics coalition – the monetarists – whose high priest is Milton Friedman. Though Reagan himself is much less dogmatically monetarist than, for example, the Thatcher government, it is ironically the monetarists who have so far achieved more of their stated policy than any other part of the coalition. And this, also ironically, is due to an appointee of President Jimmy Carter: Paul Volcker, the chairman of the Federal Reserve Board, who has turned out to be so successful at cutting the money supply that the senior members of the Reagan administration, from the President downwards, have been publicly asking him to stop.

One of their worries is that one particular aspect of his tight monetarist policies – the high interest rates – are, just as in Britain, imposing serious financial burdens on those buying a home on a mortgage or goods on hire purchase (in response to falling real wages, credit purchases have expanded rapidly in recent years in the USA). High interest rates have also led many unprofitable, debt-laden firms dangerously close to the edge of bankruptcy.

Hence in the build up to the Congressional elections of 1982 interest rates were, at least temporarily, reduced. But the problem of massive prospective government deficits remained and threatened to push interest rates up again.

There is a further item of Reaganomics on which all its factions agree – deregulation, or 'getting the Federal government off the backs of the capitalists'. Deregulation has become another euphemism for turning the whole of the USA into an enterprise zone where capital can behave in an entirely uninhibited way. For instance, it will come as a surprise to the cynical that until Reagan's 'deregulation', Federal regulations had dictated that American manufacturers could not make untrue statements in their advertising!

A much more serious aspect of deregulation is the attempt to dismantle health and safety regulations in industry. Car safety regulations have already been eased. Also the number of prosecutions initiated by the US justice department for environmental protection violations has been sharply cut back under Reagan. What dominates the administration's thinking is that at least in the short run a polluted land and an unsafe and less healthy land could be a more profitable land.

On the other hand, despite the obsession and energy which is going into cutbacks and deregulations, there remains a Grand Canyon in Reagan's America between effort and results. Reaganomics retains some credibility in the USA today, like Thatcherism in Britain, largely as a result of the confusion of its opponents and the paucity of the alternatives they have up to now devised.

The results of Reaganomics so far confirm one of the experiences of the Thatcher disaster in Britain: that no matter how hard governments of modern advanced capitalist economies try to cut government spending, it is very hard to achieve. But the Reagan administration seems to have realised, perhaps faster than Thatcher did, the profound obstacle to its programmes which is posed by 'entitlement' – the legal right to receive certain benefits such as free or subsidised health care and education, unemployment pay, old age pensions, and welfare benefits, even though these are still more limited in scope in the USA than in many European countries.

Despite the efforts of Reagan so far most of this entitlement – the essence of the so-called 'welfare state' – is still intact. Yet his programme calls for budget cuts of hundreds of billions of dollars over the next three years. This can only be done by a basic attack on all these kinds of entitlement. And that is what is now being prepared in detail by the agencies of the Federal government.

On its showing so far, Reaganomics is neither consistent monetarism, nor classic deflationism and fiscal conservatism, nor born-again militant supply-side economics. At present its contradictory and, by its own standards, incomplete policies seem headed for the same sorry fate as those of Thatcher in Britain: the aggravation of economic slump without any significant lessening in the travails of capital; the loss in this process of electoral support; and the gaining of a reputation for giving the corporations and the rich what they want while imposing cruel and unusual economic tortures on the poor.

Reaganomics soon changed from decisive and radical sounding oratory to a babel of conflicting voices from the Administration and Congressional leaders. And from the President no longer come the confident predictions of 1980 but rather vague and ambiguous conjectures – much like the astrology on which he and Nancy Reagan are said to be very dependent.

The family, the nation and race

The so-called New Right in the USA (a myriad of tiny ultra-conservative groups, many of them religious) have formed a vanguard to propagate reactionary positions on a number of non-economic issues including race, the family, the rights and role of women, homosexuality, patriotism, militarism and so on.

In the light of history these developments are not surprising. When the authority or means of existence of a ruling class have been threatened, as are those of the capitalist class today, these have all been methods commonly used in order to help turn the tide. An obvious way of strengthening the power of rulers is to foster divisions among the ruled. In the 1930s bigotry, discrimination and in the end genocide against Jews in Central Europe were used in this way. Today anti-Semitism is far from dead. But the forms of bigotry and discrimination which threaten to grow fastest are against blacks, foreigners, women, gay people and youth. Such groups are prime targets at present because of the way in which they have organised to gain more rights in the advanced countries in the boom years. A particularly common kind of demand in this respect is for the repatriation of immigrants.

Political reaction in our century has also usually gone along with the ideology of the family. When authority at the centre of society is threatened it tends to buttress itself with the most obviously available micro-unit of social discipline – the family. The aspects of the family which get stressed are the authority of men over women, and of adults over children, and restrictive sexual morality especially as applied to women and gay people.

George Gilder, from whose best seller *Poverty and Wealth* I have already quoted, attributes the current capitalist crisis to the decline of the authority of men:

> The man has the gradually sinking feeling that his role as provider, the definitive male activity from the primal days of the hunt and on into modern life, has been largely seized from him; he has been cuckolded by the compassionate state.

The American New Right has partly supported Reagan's economic policies because they seem likely to give women the maximum opportunity to return to where the New Right thinks they belong – the kitchen.

The Moral Majority and other religious groups which compose much of the New Right have have mounted a massive campaign in favour of what they see as the stabilising conservative influence of the family.

The Family Protection Act – a punitive measure with vast scope directed against the existing rights of women, minorities, youth and gays – has been introduced by supporters of the New Right in the US Congress where, along with anti-abortion legislation, it seems to be gaining ground. Even if not passed, its continual discussion contributes to a change in moral climate. Already the Moral Majority has succeeded in defeating laws at the local level in the USA which would have legalised homosexuality and liberalised other laws on sexual conduct.

Some of these same tendencies have been visible in Britain. Faced with a rebellion of especially black youth in British cities in the summer of 1981, the government of Margaret Thatcher blamed parents for their children's indiscipline. And since then Thatcher has stepped up her propaganda offensive on the value of the family, helped coincidentally by the temporary loss of a son in the Sahara desert! It isn't only the Tories who have turned to the image of the family for succour and support. In the 1979 general election the Labour Party published a special broadsheet glorifying the family by James Callaghan. And, as Prime Minister, Callaghan, in deference to the Rev. Ian Paisley's anti-gay campaign 'Save Ulster from Sodomy', withdrew a plan to legalise homosexual conduct between men in Northern Ireland. In exchange he was rewarded by the Ulster Unionists not voting against his shaky government on issues of confidence.

The various Reverends of all these extreme organisations are probably not on their way to political power. But they serve an important function, at a time when the capitalist class is in search of a radical political alternative, of shifting the centre of politics to the right and of undermining the chances of building alliances of the oppressed.

Problems of a capitalist solution

So far then it appears that although the bold-sounding new right economic experiments of Thatcherism and Reaganomics are heading for failure, and although they have caused millions of people to suffer in the process, the likelihood of a radical capitalist alternative to them in the near future is quite small.

The only other runner currently in sight is a plan based on the ideas of New York financier Felix Rohatyn. He has proposed a scheme to channel vast amounts of state funds through a kind of Industrial Reconstruction Finance Corporation to private industry to finance investment. This might be combined with the cutback of state-provided services and the implementation of wage controls and tax penalties against firms raising prices. Rohatyn used such a scheme to rescue the bankrupt New York City in the later 1970s. Grander versions of it have received support from sections of the US Democratic

Party, the British Social Democrats and influential capitalist magazines like the *Economist* and *Business Week*.

It is quite possible that this kind of relatively liberal corporatism has a future, at least as a short-term experiment. Politically it has already excited the interests of some capitalists in the USA, Britain and Europe. Some of them see it as duplicating some elements of the Japanese economic model. It also overlaps with many aspects of the alternative economic strategies now so common in the labour movement which are discussed in the final chapter of this book. So it is not impossible that a capitalist-labour alliance could build up in some countries around a modernised version of Roosevelt's New Deal.

But this Newer Deal would still have to face many of the same economic contradictions as the radical right or Keynesian solutions; and it would also have to be imposed at an obvious cost to workers. How long it could survive before colliding with these obstacles is hard to say. But it should be recalled that, contrary to a widely-held myth, it was almost certainly not the New Deal which rescued US and world capitalism from the Great Depression – but war.

What makes it so difficult for capitalist governments to come up with a set of policies which can simultaneously solve all of their problems?

The answer to that question has two parts. First of all, it is because, as we have seen, the conditions for the successful production and realisation of surplus value are themselves contradictory. For this reason no policies will unambiguously benefit all of the capital class at the same time. At a moment of acute crisis, the reversal of one aspect of economic disequilibrium may exacerbate another. As a result of this the bourgeoisie may be indecisive and erratic in its policy choices. And it may also be divided within iself according to where the balance of self-interest of its particular sections lie. This is why to break out of the stalemate the bourgeoisie requires a strategy which can transcend the special interest of its various sections. Even when a political leadership appears which seems to offer this prospect, however, such as the apparently far-sighted, confident and ruthless governments of Margaret

Thatcher and Ronald Reagan a further problem arises: can the strategy be politically implemented within the context of a bourgeois parliamentary democracy?

It is one thing to think of what to do; it is another to have the political power to carry it out in a bourgeois democratic country with trade unions, political freedoms and periodic elections. That is why a host of Reagan's early planned attacks on entitlements – such a reduction in the real level of pension and the ketchup proposal – were proposed and then later withdrawn and it became clear that they could not be carried out politically. This is an inevitable problem because, by their very nature, these policies are liable to be unpopular with large sections of the electorate. In the USA major Congressional elections take place every two years. And hardly any government in the advanced countries can expect more than four or five years of life without the need to please some of the electorate.

This difficulty was highlighted by a perceptive remark by Reagan's axeperson, David Stockman, in a notorious interview in *Atlantic Monthly* in December 1981. The budget, he soberly observed,

> isn't something you reconstruct each year. The budget is a sort of rolling history of decisons. All kinds of decisions made, five, ten, fifteen years ago, are coming back to bite us unexpectedly. Therefore, in my judgement, it will take three or four or five years to subdue it. Whether anyone can maintain the political momentum to fight the beast for that long I don't know.

Politically, fighting the beast of public spending means in reality fighting those interests which benefit from it. Up to now in Reagan's America the cutbacks have hit the least organised interests most. If there is no U-turn, then a deeper incision will strike at more organised interests – in particular the trade union movement.

The logic of Thatcherism and Reaganomics require the destruction of the kind of labour strength and solidarity which can defend jobs in the public sector and state benefits. This real dilemma points to a number of missing ingredients in government policies as they are usually conceived. Just to change state expenditure, taxation and the regulations which govern the activities of capitalism, however radically it is done, may have economically perverse results unless the government also engineers a radical shift in the balance of political power between the different classes and groups. In the main capitalist countries, in spite of the undoubted strength of right-wing governments, they have still to break decisively all the capacity for resistance which built up during the years of the postwar boom.

The implication of this is that the danger of authoritarian solutions is growing – not in the sense that there exists any fascist movements on the brink of taking power, but because the objective difficulties of resolving the crisis in a way which satisfies the needs of capital and wins elections can be expected to drive more and more of the bourgeoisie towards authoritarian non-parliamentary solutions. Already in most of the major capitalist countries, as well as most of the backward ones, the crisis is resulting in the most intense attack on many democratic rights which has been seen since the second world war. Like Norman Tebbitt in Britain, many Ministers of Labour are engaged in piloting anti-union legislation through their respective parliaments.

These are the same difficulties which are leading many of the major capitalist leaders at present to espouse militantly reactionary ideologies and policies on many questions other than the class struggle. Militarism, patriotism, racism and sexism are all in this way growing like maggots in the rotting flesh of capitalism.

Politics and economics are as hard to forecast as the weather. What seems to be the most probable expectation to emerge from this analysis is, first, that as long as the bourgeoisie maintains the reins of political power in the major capitalist countries, their governments will tend to move towards the right. But, second, they will still be forced to make periodic major concessions in order to survive politically in the context of parliamentary democracy. And third, alongside these governments, ultra-right-wing movements will continue to grow. Major clashes with workers' organisations can be expected to continue.

But in the immediate future we do not seem to be approaching an apocalyptic and historically decisive clash which will resolve the present crisis. Capitalism is heading neither straight towards the resolution of its crisis on the terms of the bourgeoisie, nor towards any final collapse. For some years to come it seems destined to continue in a state of deep and unresolved crisis, whose manifestation may change again as it has up to now.

This, however, is not a prophecy: it is a statement of what seems most likely on the basis of certain assumptions. There are other possibilities, especially if one major capitalist country breaks ranks with the others and attempts a markedly different road to the resolution of the crisis.

But if the bourgeoisie seems incapable of carrying through its own 'final solution' to the crisis – one which would involve untold further suffering for humanity – we must ask what are the possibilities of the crisis being resolved by a radical solution of the left, by a decisive move in the direction of socialism?

6.

A Socialist Horizon?

Is there another way?

In the first chapter of this book, I argued that today, perhaps for the first time in human history, economic resources and scientific knowledge were sufficient to free humanity of material want.

If destructive and wasteful production were eliminated, and if unused resources – human and material – were put to use, then enough goods and services could be produced to supply everyone on earth with a relatively comfortable standard of living. And what is more, that could almost certainly be done while at the same time permitting most people who now toil all their lives to work shorter hours, less years and under less arduous conditions than they now do.

In brief, this could be the result if the earth produced more than it does, if it produced more useful things than it does, and if they were distributed more equitably. All that is materially possible and could be done in an economy where resources were distributed not in accordance with profit or bureaucratic whim but according to real popular need.

But is it – or even an approach towards it – politically possible? Or is there nothing for it but to endure the results of the policies which various sections of the capitalists are now implementing or advocating to cope with the present crisis? Is it now possible instead to foresee a socialist solution in which it is the real needs of ordinary human beings which directly govern what is produced, how it is produced and how it is distributed, and not the requirement of capitalists to make profit or the requirements of governments to prepare for war and to control their subjects?

The answer to that question is most important in conditions of economic crisis because previous attempts to resolve major crises have led not to socialism but to sharply increased social and international conflict. The 1939–45 world war which was related to attempts to resolve the economic crisis of the 1930s led to genocide and tens of millions of hideous deaths. The equivalent aftermath of the present crisis could mean the annihilation of humanity.

Alternatives in the labour movement

A number of reformist governments have been elected in recent years in the advanced capitalist countries pledged to restore economic growth and the growth of real wages, to maintain or even improve the social services, to provide jobs for the unemployed, and carry out a host of other reforms with important economic consequences.

And yet virtually all such governments have abandoned these promises and ended up cutting government spending, imposing credit squeezes, trying to curtail wages and implementing other elements of an all too familiar list. In Britain the Labour governments of Callaghan and Wilson are perfect examples of this. The Mitterrand government in France now seems to be travelling a similar path.

Such failures have paved the way for the more thoroughgoing and open right-wing attacks now being mounted by Thatcher and Reagan.

But the failure of the traditional parties of the working class to offer any solution to the crisis and its problems in practice has had the effect of somewhat polarising the political discussion of economic issues within the labour movement. It has led socialists to present new schemes to combat the effects of the crisis in conflict not only with Reaganomics and Thatcherism and the like but also with the bankrupt policies of the failed leadership of the major workers' parties.

That is particularly true of the labour movement in Britain where the failure of the traditional reformist leaders in office has been most graphic. A new set of policies under the general title of the Alternative Economic Strategy (AES) has been developed by the Trades Union Congress and politicians and intellectuals in the left of the Labour Party. The AES has been particularly associated with the current of the Labour Party supporting Tony Benn. But for want of any coherent alternative and in the light of their previous failures, the centre and even some right-wing segments of the party had had to pay lip-service to it as well. In many other countries, too, very similar packages of policies are now being advocated by important sections of the labour movement.

The main features of these sets of policies are individually not very new. They consist of five main themes:

First, the expansion of government spending in total – usually concentrated on the extension of public and social services, job creation schemes of public works and involving (in the case of Britain) the reduction of defence expenditure;

Second, the nationalisation of major sectors of capital, sometimes including the main commercial banks (in order to give the government control over the direction of investment) and large manufacturing and commercial companies; it is usually implied that these nationalisations will be carried out with compensation, though the level is never made explicit in advance;

Third, the institution of measures of state economic planning, usually involving some kinds of tripartite agreements between government planning agencies, bosses (capitalists or nationalised industry leaders) and labour;

Fourth, the reduction of normal working hours. In particular the implementation of the 35-hour week;

Fifth, various measures aimed at reducing the vulnerability of the national economy to outside pressures and influences; these include controls on the activities of multinational corporations, controls on capital movements, especially foreign investment by home-based multinationals, along with various protectionist measures such as import controls, exchange rate devaluation and so on.

This list is not exhaustive. The way it is presented above is very much influenced by the Alternative Economic Strategy which has been widely canvassed in the British Labour Party and trade union movement. But the original plans of the Mitterrand government in France were not so different. And very closely related policies are being advocated on the left throughout Europe and even in the United States.

Are these policies a real and practicable alternative at the present time? Will they resolve the crisis and restore the health of the world economy? Are they socialist? These and related questions must be examined very closely in the labour movement. Yet so far the alternative strategy and the theories behind it have met with a relatively uncritical reception.

The rest of this chapter, therefore is an attempt to produce a socialist critique of these alternative policies.

Problems of the new Keynesianism

Common to all version of the AES is the demand for a reversal of cuts in public expenditure and an expansion of state spending to end the recession and to create jobs, as well as to restore and improve public services. All of these are aims which obviously deserve strong support.

But on closer examination the policies appear much more problematic. This partly comes from the fact that they were based on a very superficial analysis of the source of the problem. Cuts in public spending made by right-wing governments tend to be attributed to errors or pure vindictiveness on the part of the capitalist class. Advocates of the alternative strategies often speak as if the present recessions and cutbacks just resulted from the policies of governments such as those of Thatcher, Giscard or Reagan.

Of course, their policies have exacerbated the problem. But they are not policies out of the blue. They are a response to the decline in profitability which capitalism has suffered. They are part of an attempt to reverse the forces which have produced that decline and start afresh.

We have seen that the interests of the capitalists are not

simple and unambiguous because of the contradictory conditions which exist for the production and realisation of profit (surplus value). For this reason some sections of capital still favour high government spending. And up until very recently some capitalist governments themselves were still advocating policies of spending their way out of the crisis. The fact is, however, that these policies produced other problems – inflation, uncontrollable state deficits and so on – which helped to lead to the present domination of monetarism, supply-side economics and the like.

Too often the advocates of the alternative strategy fail even to register that such problems might exist.

Traditional Keynesian policies of spending one's way out of a crisis have been abandoned by the leading sections of the capitalist class at present because they did not resolve the problems of the capitalist class and in some ways made them worse. Unless the left knows why such problems have occurred with Keynesianism and has a plan to deal with them, then high spending policies will lead again to the same results. And there is good reason to think that, since the profitability crisis has continued to deepen, the contradictions of Keynesianism will appear more rapidly the next time it is tried.

They have not taken long to appear in France. When the Mitterand government came into office in 1981 it set out at once to direct a stagnant French economy back towards expansion and full employment. Minimum wages and social security payments were increased; emphasis was placed on the expansion of government spending and the deficit accordingly grew as all good Keynesians would say it should.

At the end of a year real wages had gone up. But so had unemployment; and production after a brief burst of energy was once again stagnant. But inflation, the government deficit and the balance of payments deficit were all rising fast and looked to be out of control. French inflation was running at 9 per cent a year more than in neighbouring West Germany and two devaluations of the franc had been necessary to keep French products competitive in European markets.

At this point in mid-1982 the government began to eat its

expansionist words. Prices and wages were frozen for four months; social security contributions were raised; proposed increases in family allowances and pensions were postponed; and several items of government spending, including hospital building, were cut back. Ministers began calling for financial discipline and their words took on a distinctly more protectionist tinge. So the new lease of life of Keynesian expansionism in France turned out to be very brief.

Many supporters of the alternative strategy still have little awareness of the kinds of problems which gave rise to the French economic emergency of 1982. Those who have considered the problem can give various answers. In reply to the fear that more state spending will be very inflationary, they can reply that they will control prices. In theory this is possible, although it implies that inflation will then take a different form, that of unsatisfied demands for goods. To prevent unsatisfied demand being that of the most deserving consumers, price controls can in theory be supplemented by rationing. In practice such a state of affairs has existed in a number of 'planned socialist economies' such as Cuba and Poland, as well as in wartime capitalist countries. One result is invariably corruption, profiteering, black markets on a grand scale – and bureaucratic inefficiency and injustice. So, even if these measures were taken, the result might not be a democratically planned economy but rather a combination of an economic police state, and private gangsterism. Furthermore, price controls imply wage controls or state subsidies if they are not to lead to a wave of bankruptcies of private firms.

Some defenders of the alternative strategy argue instead that the inflationary consequences of more state spending can be overcome by financing the new spending by higher taxes on capital. The most widely proposed measure of this kind is the imposition of a wealth tax, or the tightening of the many tax loopholes from which capitalists benefit. The problem with this, however, is that wealth taxes are notoriously easy for the propertied classes to avoid paying, while other forms of taxation on capital are virtually ruled out on the scale proposed because of the fall in profitability which has taken place.

Unfortunately, very few of the advocates of the alternative strategy are prepared to look seriously at the problems which state spending would produce. They prefer to treat it as a kind of magic wand. Theoretically they don't get beyond a very crude form of Keynesianism which has long been exposed in practice as being insufficient to explain or resolve the economic crisis. And politically their strategy fails to prepare its supporters for difficult situations which would arise very quickly if this part of the alternative strategy were implemented with vigour.

It would only be possible to begin to deal with the problems of rising state expenditure at present by combining it with other policies which make major inroads into the rights of capitalist property owners and other policies directed towards mass democratic involvement in economic life. And that, of course, means a political strategy to defend any reforms that are made by stronger means than those legally permitted by bourgeois parliamentary democracy.

Problems of nationalisation and planning

Advocates of the alternative strategy do try partly, however, to overcome these objections by linking their policy of state spending to a policy of nationalisation of the banks and big industry. There are three main problems with this if it is to be an element in a socialist solution of the economic crisis. One is the question of compensation. If capitalists are 'fairly' compensated for their assets with money or state bonds then measures of nationalisation do not imply lessening in the degree of capitalist exploitation but merely a change in the way in which the exploitation of the working class takes place. The state will still be obliged to raise the surplus value with which to continue to compensate the capitalists, though that would be done indirectly through taxation. Capitalists in the past have often agreed to nationalisation, even of profitable companies, when they have received adequate compensation. But to give less than 'adequate compensation' implies measures of a much more revolutionary character than seems to be contemplated by any of the advocates of the alternative strategies. In France, for example, the owners of the banks nationalised in 1981 were certainly not ungenerously compensated.

The second problem associated with nationalisation is the organisation of industries after they have been nationalised. In the past nationalised industries in the capitalist countries have been run as vast centralised bureaucracies in which the relations of the workers with their work and their employers has been not a scrap different from those in a capitalist-owned corporation. They have been a form of state capitalism. Increasingly the tendency has been for governments to insist that all nationalised industries make a profit on the same basis as capitalist companies and this has made them even more alien to their workers and the users of their products.

Nationalisation can imply a step towards a more just and socialist economy. But only if it allows really radical steps to be taken towards replacing production for profit with production based on social need. And that would require not putting workers' representatives on remote, centralised boards of management but real workers' and users' control of the industries and their resources. Again that is a situation far more radical politically than most of the advocates of the alternative strategy propose.

Again the alternative strategists have what they present as a partial answer to this – economic planning. But the kind of planning they often appear to envisage is a very centralised, bureaucratic affair in which ordinary workers and consumers could play little part. There are also major elements of left corporatism in their strategy in that they want to organise planning through agreements between capitalists' and workers' and state representatives which will involve a sacrifice of workers' independence in order to persuade capitalists to behave according to the plan.

But it has been proved many times that capitalists cannot be forced to plan in accordance with the needs of workers and consumers. They are in business to make profits and will take any action which they think necessary to succeed in that. The advocates of the alternative strategy, however, seem to envisage the real prospect of a planned mixed economy in which capitalists would agree to coordinate their investment, pricing and employment decisions with the needs of a left-wing government.

In practice it is much more likely that any attempt to implement the alternative strategy, even with all its limitations, would still be regarded by the capitalists as a very major threat to their existence as a class. Even if they recognised the very moderate intentions of many of the leading advocates of the strategy, they would fear the stimulus which the implementation of the strategy might spark off within ordinary people and popular and working-class movements. They would not be clamouring to make agreements but rather organising to undermine the defeat of any progressive policies which the government seriously tried to implement.

Less work, more jobs?

The last point applies especially to the demand which many see as the 'easiest' of the alternative strategies – the proposal for a 35-hour week which has united the whole of the Western European trade unions. Put at its crudest the proposal says that cutting the working week by one-eighth would increase the number of jobs by one-eighth and so get rid of unemployment.

If that's the idea, and assuming no cut in pay for the shorter hours, then the proposal clearly hasn't got a snowball in hell's chance as long as capitalism remains in its present critical condition. Some of its advocates realise this and present it as an alternative to wage increases, or in combination with wage cuts. In this form it can become a demand which capitalists might be able to exploit to their advantage, through most will oppose it because it would tend to reduce the reserve army of labour.

So any demand related to hours, if it is not to be sugar coating on the pill of wage cuts and speed-up, needs to be presented very unambiguously, making clear that it assumes no compromise on wages and that, because of its anti-capitalist content, it needs to be combined with other anti-capitalist measures to have a chance of success. When the Mitterrand govern-

ment reduced the working week in 1981 from 40 to 39 hours a
series of bitter struggles were needed before it was generally
established that the reduction should be without loss of pay. A
reduction to 35 hours would obviously provoke a much more
ferocious opposition. Nonetheless, reduction of hours without
loss of pay is an essential part of any socialist programme in two
senses. First, it is a way of protecting jobs during a depression
so in this sense it is a work-sharing demand. As such, a blanket
35-hour week proposal, though it can be an important focus of
national and international political struggle, is insufficient and
needs to be supplemented by specific work-sharing demands in
individual workplaces. Second, demands for reducing work
hours are an important part of a programme which goes
beyond the defence of existing living standards. It is a necessary
precondition for the expansion of leisure and the fuller development of the human individual which will be possible in a
socialist society.

From the middle of the nineteenth century the length of the
standard working week fell in advanced capitalist countries
until the 40-hour week was generally established after the
second world war. Since then it has hardly changed despite the
growth of unions. If historical trends had continued it would be
now have been down almost to 30 hours. So, taking a long-
term view, a 30-hour week would not be an unreasonable
demand for today.

Nationalism and internationalism

The British advocates of the alternative strategy tend to be very
selective in the future problems they see. If they on the whole
underestimate the internal economic contradictions of their
strategy and the dangers to it from national capitalist counter-
action, they are on the other hand ultra-sensitive to threats to it
from abroad.

In many versions of the strategy multinational corporations
are elevated to the great villains of the world economy. The
proponents are apt to talk less of the problems of *capitalist*
domination of the economy than of the problems of *foreign*

capitalist domination. There is a general bias against foreign capitalist investment which is not directed against capitalist investment in general. Quite the contrary: the home-based capitalists are often accused of being unpatriotic by investing overseas instead of at home.

It is, of course, easy to see why from the narrow perspective of a bureaucatically conceived national government this should seem to be a problem. To the worker, however, it can hardly be said to matter whether she or he is exploited by British, Japanese or American capital. The problem for workers is not to be able to exercise control over a limited area of the world economy, but rather to have a secure source of income, a better life and more choice and independence.

The AES supporters advocate nationalist policies not only in relation to investment, but also pre-eminently in relation to trade. They recognise that one of the problems of rising state spending and economic recovery may be the rapid growth of imports which they plan to deal with by import controls to afford protection to national industries while they improve their efficiency and competitiveness.

Like their approach to state spending this aspect of the alternative strategy is also classically Keynesian. During the crisis of the 1930s Keynes was an advocate, not only of Britain spending its way out of the slump, but also of protecting its way out of the slump.

Since most of the advocates of the alternative strategy claim to be socialists, and since socialists usually claim to be internationalist, it is not surprising that it is these nationalistic aspects of the strategy which have aroused most criticism. Their advocates have been more defensive about them than about other parts of the strategy. In Britain many of the supporters of the strategy have stopped talking about import controls and employ various euphemisms like 'planned growth of trade', which they say will benefit other countries.

But for all these mouth-fresheners, there is something fundamentally foul-smelling about policies which in the name of socialism try to improve the lot of workers in one country at the expense of those in another.

The basic objection to nationalistic protectionist policies, however, is not a moral one, nor the obvious fact that they may be self-defeating because they provoke retaliation. It is rather that politically they are suicidal for any socialist strategy. Any radical anti-capitalist economic measures in a single country will provoke not only domestic but international retaliation. That is because the capitalists are an international class, and never more so than today. The insular and chauvinistic tendencies of alternative economic strategies has meant that their main advocates have deservedly failed to gain recognition as leaders of a new movement towards world socialism as a solution to the increasingly devastating economic crisis.

Unfortunately, the alternative strategy is frequently conceived as one for a government in a single country. Insofar as it looks for support outside the country it is not to the mass movement that it foresees appealing but rather to other governments. This too is a potentially fatal weakness.

Socialism which is not conceived internationally is both meaningless and impracticable. Anti-capitalist measures in one country, if they remain isolated there, will in the long run be defeated or converted into measures which are no longer anti-capitalist. The history of socialism in one country in the USSR is an appalling demonstration of that. The leaders of that country have for years helped to uphold capitalism and exploitation around the world.

The workers of one country trying to impose anti-capitalist measures can only ask for the necessary practical support of the workers of other countries if they show that what they are doing is not conceived of as pursuing national self-interest but rather the interest of all the working class and oppressed and deprived people against the exploiters and the privileged.

Socialists must urgently devise a truly, internationalist policy. That means setting ourselves against protectionism. It means striving for more and more contact and consultation with the international working-class and anti-imperialist movements about policies in any one country where an anti-capitalist government takes power. It also means building these contacts before the event. It means placing the needs of the backward underdeveloped countries in the forefront of our concerns instead of saying, as so many advocates of the alternative strategy do, that they have to wait for assistance until we have solved our problems.

We must fight for support for the unconditional cancellation of the vast debts of the poor countries to the international banks and to imperialist governments. We must demand the ending of economic discrimination against the exports of the poor countries. We should advocate a massive programme of economic aid aimed at helping the poor countries. For this aid to be practically useful we should call for it to be directed towards governments that take serious anti-capitalist measures in their own countries and towards national liberation movements in the still-oppressed nations.

In the advanced countries, especially, internationalism requires a commitment against immigration controls – support, in American terminology, for 'open borders'. If the people of the advanced countries are able to gain some of the benefits of socialism they will have no interest in converting them into their exclusive property.

If socialists are serious that these are high among our priorities, then we shall be able to build stronger alliances with progressive forces representing the oppressed people of the underdeveloped countries. And that will make the struggle for socialism there and also in advanced countries like Britain an easier one.

Socialism and parliament

The alternative strategy tends to be almost exclusively conceived as one for a national *government*. This means it systematically underplays the role of independent mobilisation of workers, consumers, women and other sections of the population around their own interests. The implied political role of the people is not to take direct action to further their own interests which any left government would then do everything possible to defend, but rather the opposite – to mobilise only in defence of the actions of the government, but otherwise to remain passive and grateful recipients of the reforms.

Beyond that the strategy is conceived of as one for a government not only legally elected through bourgeois democracy, but also, once elected, adhering to all the rules of bourgeois legality on the assumption that everyone else, including those threatened by reforms, will adhere to all such rules. But history has shown over and over again that, as soon as their interests are regarded as seriously threatened, the property-owning classes would have no compunction in abandoning the rules of bourgeois legality. If the possibility of reform is not to vanish, as in Germany in 1933, or Spain in 1936, or Chile in 1973, then any alternative strategy needs to be backed by a political mobilisation which challenges the straitjacket into which bourgeois parliamentary democracy aims to confine mass politics. New representative and democratic organs of rule will have to be built in factories, schools, offices and neighbourhoods.

Socialists often wrongly decry the use of parliament to achieve or reinforce necessary reforms. In fact it is the most reformist forces who are most timid in the use of parliament because they realise that any seriously legislated anti-capitalist measures can be enforced only through extra-parliamentary mobilisation.

Socialists should advocate a much more audacious and energetic use of parliament by parties which claim to represent the working class. It is very important therefore for any future labour or socialist government to be equipped with a coherent programme of economic measures which it will use its power as a national government to implement. But this cannot be the exclusive aim and activity of socialists.

A truly socialist strategy should approach the problem of how to confront the crisis from a different starting point than that of most alternative strategies. It does not begin by assuming the election of a left parliamentary government. It begins from the question of what the working class and other oppressed sections of the population can do on all fronts and in alliance with each other to combat the economic and political problems which they face as a result of the capitalist crisis.

This means, for example, that it includes policies within the labour movement for the day-to-day struggle to protect real wages and defend jobs at the level of industries, firms and factories. That will in many cases mean local strikes and occupations supported by solidarity action elsewhere.

In relation to the declining social services, too, many actions can be taken, as in many cases they have been, to defend threatened services like schools and hospitals. It must be made as difficult as possible for right-wing governments to impose their policies.

Faced with redundancies and lay-offs, a socialist strategy should include the sharing out of work available among the existing workforce in order to prevent redundancies; and opposition to any wage cuts or work speed-up which employers might try to introduce.

It is obvious from the worsening position of women and oppressed racial and other minorities in the advanced countries mentioned earlier, that a socialist programme to deal with the crisis must contain many measures designed to deal with the problems of these specific groups, the right to a job for women and for youth and the ending of all discrimination in employment practices against women, youth, blacks and gay people.

Feminist writers have pointedly observed that most versions of the alternative economic strategy devised in the male-dominated labour movement have systematically failed to take account of the independent needs of women. It is not only that they omit or give insufficient prominence to demands which affect women's lives – equal pay, equal job opportunities, rights to unemployment and other benefits, the provision of child care facilities, abortion and other rights; it is also that the strategy is often conceived in the framework of very conservative thinking about social life. Its demands rest on numerous unspoken assumptions that workers always live in nuclear families for which men are expected to earn a family wage and women are expected to carry out housework and child care.

Just because the alternative strategy which is now so popular within the labour movement has all the limitations which I have tried to outline, does not mean that socialists should abstain from the struggle over the policies of the labour and socialist parties and the trade unions. To do that would be sectarian and would contribute to the weakness of the right for socialism.

In Britain, I believe that socialists should be in the forefront of the debate over what policies a future Labour government should pursue. And this would apply to other countries where political parties of the working class have a chance of gaining power.

There are many policies within the authorised versions of alternative strategies which deserve strong support: for instance, more government spending to restore and improve the social services, a programme of useful public works to create jobs for the millions of unemployed, the reduction of working hours (provided it is without loss of pay), nationalisation – though without compensation to large capitalists and giving paramount importance to the workers' control of nationalised industries.

We also have to fight to see that the political needs and consequences of any anti-capitalist policies are fully realised and prepared for by the whole labour movement. If everything is left to representatives in parliament then it will fail. Every real reform or anti-capitalist measure made by legislation or government action needs protection by mass mobilisation.

Out of that need come two further important questions: first, how to combat the ever-present military threat to socialism; and second, what political alliance is capable of finding a way out of the present crisis towards a better society?

Against militarism

Any socialist struggle for better economic conditions and greater democracy is doomed unless it is linked to a fight against militarism. On numerous counts the vast expenditure which now takes place on the ability to destroy human beings in all countries constitutes a primary obstacle to socialist goals.

First, perhaps as much as $1 trillion ($250 for every woman, man and child on earth) is spent in the world each year on military purposes. This simply subtracts from the resources which could in principle be used to supply real human needs instead of the means of destruction.

Second, historical experience has shown that the existence of standing armies is a permanent threat to radical reform in both capitalist and 'socialist' countries. Any actions or government policies which seriously threaten the ability to exploit workers and other oppressed groups are vulnerable to military coups. Everywhere military rule is the reserve power of the exploiting ruling classes and groups, for use when politics, ideology and the law fail them. And military power usually means not just a halt to reform but the destruction of all the forces and organisations committed to reform. This is why no really anti-capitalist struggle can restrict itself to observing the norms of bourgeois legality when these are being violated by the bourgeoisie itself. Obviously a socialist programme for this reason cannot restrict itself to abstract calls for disarmament but must include measures to prevent military leaders from being able to use their power – in other words measures to integrate rank-and-file soldiers with the overall struggle for reform.

Third, disarmament is an integral part of an internationalist strategy. The unilateral disarmament of the rich and powerful countries would be the strongest possible confirmation that they offer no threat to the economic or political interest of other nations. It would serve to underline and confirm any internationalist intentions expressed by left governments.

Finally, talk of economic advancement and equality, of social and political justice, sounds hollow and utopian against the background of a world which is armed to the teeth. It is almost impossible to believe that a destructive capacity estimated to be able to eliminate humanity many times over will not some time be used. For all these reasons any socialist movement in the advanced countries worthy of its name must embrace unilateral disarmament. It is a demand directed simultaneously against economic waste, against undemocratic generals, against national chauvinism and against world destruction.

An anti-capitalist alliance

The kind of strategy or programme which is needed to fight the consequences of the capitalist crisis does not come from the imagination of leaders or intellectuals. It is an amalgam of the real demands of all those whose economic, political and personal needs are not being met by the present exploitative capitalist system or its existing 'socialist' alternative.

Politically, therefore, it implies an alliance of organisations, movements and individuals which combat oppression – of workers against economic hardship and workplace oppression, of minorities against racial discrimination and prejudice, of the people of poor countries for their national liberation and for economic development in democratic conditions, of young unemployed against the failure of capitalism to offer them any future, of women against their double oppression in today's society, of lesbians and gay men against our nearly universal social oppression.

I do not believe that the need for such a broad alliance at the present time is just a left-wing political platitude. It springs from an immediate danger to all those groups – a danger which results from what the rulers and exploiting classes of the world are being driven to do in an effort to resolve the current crisis by restoring the flow of profit, their lifeblood. That does not mean that the origin of all forms of political, social, racial or sexual oppression are economic or are linked in a very mechanical way with the state of the economy. Patriarchy, sexism and racism for instance existed long before capitalism and will no doubt outlast it. And they exist in both boom and crisis.

The major focus of this book has of course been narrowly economic. But I have tried to show that all forms of oppression are linked in some way to economic factors. And in particular that conditions of severe economic crisis tend to intensify and to increase the links between all forms of oppression in that they give the exploiting classes a reason to tighten every screw, to worsen the political conditions for all kinds of progressive struggle and to attempt to divide the protagonists of different struggles. That is why all oppressed people in today's society are likely to suffer more, and not just in terms of their economic conditions, when an economic crisis breaks out.

A broad alliance of oppressed and exploited people, however, is not only prevented by divisions fostered by the ruling class. Many of them come from sectarianism and bigotry within those movements themselves. Within the traditionally powerful labour movement, an absolutely necessary leading element in an effective anti-capitalist movement, lurk many reactionary positions on questions like democracy, racism, nationalism, sexism and homophobia – such positions exist even in parts of the movement which are most progressive on many economic questions. The ideas of the enemy can multiply in the minds of potential allies. Ideological germ warfare can be as effective as tanks and stormtroopers, though they often go together. So a big part of the job of building an anti-capitalist alliance consists in fighting prejudice and the lack of democracy in the organisations which must compose it.

In the 1930s the necessary anti-capitalist alliance was never constructed. At the crucial moments the progressive forces were weakened either by inter-party sectarianism or by too narrow a conception of the struggle. But the reactionary camp of those times was by contrast able to advance on all fronts together. The need for a broad, democratic and anti-capitalist alliance is today as strong as it was then. The difference is that this time the consequence of not building it may not merely be the barbaric horrors of the 1930s and 1940s. It may be literally the death of humanity. This may be the last chance ever to ensure that the horizon is not as dark as it appears today.

A Guide to Reading

One of the best ways to gain a very detailed but accessible idea of the present state of the world economy is to read an annual publication of the World Bank called *World Development Report*. Most of the information in Chapter 2 came from here and it is a particularly useful source of economic information on the third world.

On 7 September 1982 *The Financial Times* published a valuable and informative supplement on 'The World Economy'. Continuously updated surveys of the world economy are published in the *Quarterly Bulletin* of the Bank of England, in the *National Institute Economic Review* (also quarterly) and *Economic Outlook*, published every six months by the OECD.

There is a readable account of the long postwar boom from a more or less Keynesian point of view in Angus Maddison's *Economic Growth in the West*, New York: Twentieth Century Fund 1964. A briefer account from a marxist point of view can be found in Andrew Glyn and John Harrison, *The British Economic Disaster*, Pluto Press 1980. Other marxist accounts of the postwar boom can be found in Paul Baran and Paul Sweezy, *Monopoly Capital*, Penguin 1968, in Ernest Mandel, *Late Capitalism*, New Left Books 1975, and in Andre Gunder Frank, *Crisis in the World Economy*, Heinemann 1980.

On the development of the economic role of the state in the postwar period thre are two very good books by marxists: James O'Connor's *The Fiscal Crisis of the State*, St.Martin's Press 1973, and Ian Gough's *The Political Economy of the*

Welfare State, Macmillan 1979.

There is a long and interesting review of Gough's book by John Harrison: 'State Expenditure and Capital', *Cambridge Journal of Economics*, Vol.4 No.2.

Numerous marxist accounts of the current economic crisis have now been published and the following is a selection: Andrew Glyn and John Harrison, *The British Economic Disaster*, a readable and original account which concentrated on the British economy; Andre Gunder Frank, *Crisis in the World Economy* and *Crisis in the Third World*, Heinemann 1980 and 1981, a lengthy account which is particularly useful as a source of ideas of economists, politicians and the media on the crisis; Ernest Mandel, *The Second Slump*, New Left Books 1978, a shorter, more empirical and more readable book than the same author's *Late Capitalism*, analysing the crisis up to the mid-1970s; a series of essays from *Monthly Review* is published as Harry Magdoff and Paul Sweezy, *The Deepening Crisis of US Capitalism*, Monthly Review Press 1981.

Non-marxist writers took longer to wake up to the current crisis but have now begun to write about it in books such as Lester Thurow, *The Zero-sum Economy*, Penguin 1981.

Some of the contributions to the debate between marxists on the cause of the crisis and the fall in the rate of profit are Andrew Glyn and Bob Sutcliffe, *British Capitalism, Workers and the Profits Squeeze*, Penguin 1972; David Yaffe and Paul Bullock, 'Inflation, the Crisis and the Post-war Boom', which appeared in *Revolutionary Communist* No. 3/4; Andrew Gamble and Paul Walton, *Capitalism and Crisis, Inflation and the State*, Macmillan 1976, and in many issues of the *Bulletin* of the Conference of Socialist Economics (now *Capital and Class*) between 1974 and 1979.

A number of other books deal with particular aspects of the economic crisis:
on inflation see Robert Rowthorn, *Capitalism, Conflict and Inflation*, Lawrence and Wishart 1980;
on international economic and in particular monetary relations between the great capitalist powers see Ricardo Parboni, *The Dollar and Its Rivals*, New Left Books 1981; Union of Radical

Political Economics, *US Capitalism in Crisis*, 2nd edition, New York: URPE 1978, which is a useful book of readings; on the crisis of state expenditure, see Union of Radical Political Economics, Economics Education Project, *Crisis in the Public Sector*, URPE/Monthly Review Press 1982.

A number of journals publish regular articles by marxists or others of the left about aspects of the economic crisis: *Capital and Class* (journal of the Conference of Socialist Economists, Britain); *Review of Radical Political Economics* (journal of the Union of Radical Political Economics, USA); *Monthly Review*, New York; *The Socialist Review*, USA; *Labour Research*, Britain; *Dollars and Sense*, USA.

Up-to-date information on the development of the economic crisis can only be obtained from regular journals and papers such as *The Financial Times*, *The Wall Street Journal*, *Business Week*, *The Economist*. Needless to say, their outlook is anything but marxist on these questions, but they are indispensable.

Those newspapers and periodicals are also the best sources for information and commentary on the policies being pursued by capitalist governments to combat the crisis. There are two recent readable books on Reaganomics by Robert Lekachman, *Greed Is Not Enough: Reaganomics*, New York: Pantheon 1982 and by Frank Ackerman, *Reaganomics: Rhetoric vs Reality*, Pluto Press 1982). A good general discussion of the economic ideas of the American right can be found in James T. Campen and Arthur MacEwan, 'Crisis, Contradictions and Conservative Controversies in Contemporary US Capitalism', *Cambridge Journal of Economics*, 1982.

There is a discussion about the logic of Thatcherite economic policies by John Harrison in *Marxism Today*, July 1982 ('Thatcherism, Is It working?'). Some of the origins of the Thatcherite ideas are critically outlined in Andrew Gamble, *Britain in Decline*, Macmillan 1981.

One of the possible new New Deal alternatives mentioned in Chapter 5 is outlined in a long article called 'The Reindustrialisation of America', which appeared in *Business Week*, 30 June 1980.

A sympathetic but not completely uncritical account of the Alternative Economic Strategy in Britain is given in *The Alternative Economic Strategy: A Labour Movement Response to the Economic Crisis* by the London Working Group of the Conference of Socialist Economics, CSE Books, Labour Coordinating Committee 1980. There is also a lot of discussion of the AES in issues 1 and 2 of *Socialist Economic Review*, Merlin Press, 1981 and 1982. In the 1982 issue several articles discuss its deficiencies in relation to the needs of women. The AES has also been discussed in recent issues of *Capital and Class*, the *New Socialist* and *Marxism Today*.

Finally, a word on the sources of the many statistics used in this book. My main sources have been the World Bank *World Development Report* 1981 and 1982; OECD *Historical Statistics, 1960–1980*, Paris 1982; OECD *Economic Outlook*; and the regular statistical series published in *The Financial Times*. On state expenditure some of the figures come from Ian Gough's *The Political Economy of the Welfare State*, Macmillan, 1979 and on the rate of profit and long-term rates of growth from Andrew Glyn and John Harrison's *The British Economic Disaster*, Pluto Press 1980. The most recent figures on profits, productivity and investment were personally and generously supplied to me by Andrew Glyn and appear in his paper in National Institute of Economic and Social Research, *Slow Growth in the Western World*, Heinemann 1982.

On the labour force and foreign investment many figures are from Sam Aaronovitch and Ron Smith with Jean Gardiner and Roger Moore, *The Political Economy of British Capitalism, A Marxist Analysis*, McGraw Hill 1981; other figures on foreign investment came from United Nations, *Transnational Corporations in World Development*, 1978; and on international financial markets from Robert Cohen 'Structural Change in International Banking and Its Implications for the US Economy', Joint Committee of US Congress, 7 December 1980; on unemployment some figures come from K. G. Knight, 'The Composition of Unemployment', *Socialist Economic Review* 1981 and from Andre Gunder Frank, *Crisis in the World Economy*, Heinemann 1980.

Other facts and figures come from many sources including *The Wall Street Journal, The New York Times, The Washington Post, Business Week, Dollars and Sense*, the UK *Department of Employment Gazette, British Business* (published by the UK Department of Industry).